Taunton's

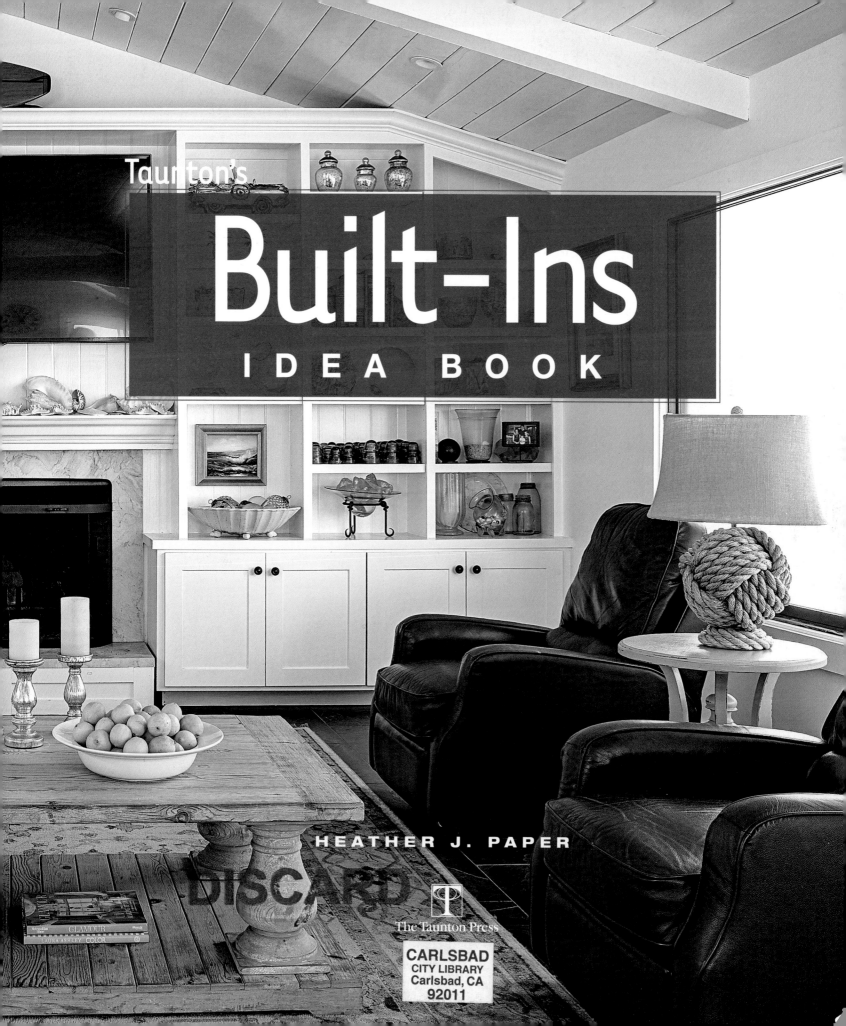

Taunton's

Built-Ins
IDEA BOOK

HEATHER J. PAPER

The Taunton Press

To my husband and best friend, Russ

The Taunton Press
Inspiration for hands-on living®

The Taunton Press, Inc.
63 South Main Street, PO Box 5506
Newtown, CT 06470-5506
e-mail: tp@taunton.com

Editors: Christina Glennon, Peter Chapman
Copy editor: Candace B. Levy
Cover design: Kim Adis
Interior design: Kim Adis
Layout: Sandra Mahlstedt
Illustrator: Joanne Kellar Bouknight
Front cover photographers: Tria Giovan (left), Mark Lohman (top right), Stacy Bass (bottom right)
Back cover photographers: Andrea Rugg (top right), Ryann Ford (center right), Mark Lohman (bottom left), Stacy Bass (bottom center)

The following names/manufacturers appearing in *Built-Ins Idea Book* are trademarks: Academy Awards® and National Kitchen & Bath Association℠

Library of Congress Cataloging-in-Publication Data

Names: Paper, Heather J., author.
Title: Built-ins idea book / author: Heather J. Paper.
Description: Newtown, CT : The Taunton Press, Inc., [2017]
Identifiers: LCCN 2017007167 | ISBN 9781631866555
Subjects: LCSH: Built-in furniture. | Interior decoration. | Cabinetwork. | Storage in the home.
Classification: LCC NK2712 .P37 2017 | DDC 645/.4--dc23
LC record available at https://lccn.loc.gov/2017007167

Printed in the United States of America
10 9 8 7 6 5 4 3 2 1

acknowledgments

acknowledging all of the people who played a role in the *Built-Ins Idea Book* is rather like an acceptance speech at the Academy Awards®. You hope you won't, inadvertently, forget anyone.

At the top of the list is what I refer to as my "A-Team" at The Taunton Press, starting with Executive Editor Peter Chapman. The confidence and support he bestowed on me every step of the way was appreciated beyond words.

My sincere thanks go as well to Christina Glennon; every writer should have an editor who's so easy to work with—and, with her spot-on edits, makes you look so good. And as you'll see from paging through this book, the photographs are just as important as the written words; I'm convinced there's not a more organized art director—with a fine eye for design—than Rosalind Loeb. My thanks go to Katy Binder, too, for keeping track of such a massive number of photographs.

Those responsible for this book also include numerous others, including the professionals represented on these pages. The creativity of builders, contractors, interior designers, and craftsmen is translated into built-ins of all shapes and sizes, resulting in rooms that are truly one of a kind.

A huge shout-out goes, too, to the photographers who provided extraordinary images for this book. Special thanks go to Chipper Hatter, Hulya Kolabas, Mark Lohman, Andrea Rugg, and Kathryn Russell for investing their time and effort to locate extraordinary examples of built-ins. But kudos go to others as well; please see the credits at the back of the book for the names of the photographers and design professionals for individual images.

Finally, I want to thank my family and friends, who are endlessly supportive—especially my husband, Russ, whose love and encouragement mean more than he will ever know.

contents

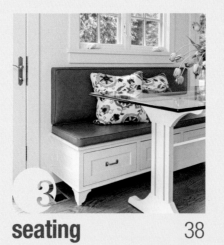

introduction

CLEARLY REMEMBER THE DAY I was asked to write the *Built-Ins Idea Book*. Admittedly, my first thought was "Is there enough to be said about built-ins to fill an entire book?" It didn't take much research, however, to be convinced. How did I conduct that "scientific" research? I simply walked through the rooms of my own home.

A quick overview of my kitchen, for instance, revealed a wealth of built-ins. Cabinets, drawers, and shelves—the essence of any kitchen—define style, shape the space, and generally elevate my kitchen's efficiency. I'd never really thought about how the built-in eating bar acts as a divider between the kitchen proper and the breakfast room. Likewise, I'd taken the built-in pantry

for granted, giving little consideration as to how the carefully arranged shelves provide a great deal of convenience. And I've long been considering built-in banquette seating; it's what I gravitate to in any restaurant, so why shouldn't I have it in my own home?

Another change I've been contemplating is the addition of built-in bookshelves in my family room, and the examples in this book have only furthered my resolve. Because I'm a writer, you can only imagine the library I've amassed, and all of those books need a home. But the thought of creating built-in storage—with enough space for books as well as collectibles, electronics, and treasured family photos—makes the idea even more attractive.

Upon entering my bedroom, one element in particular struck me immediately—the walk-in closet. The his and her storage space, fitted with wire shelving, is the ultimate built-in. It's a perfectly good solution, but I have to confess: Inspired by some of the amazing closets in this book, I may have to take it to the next level. Floor-to-ceiling shoe racks? Drawers specifically designed for jewelry and accessories? Clear-fronted doors that allow you to see the contents within while keeping dust at bay? Yes, please—to all of it.

The biggest surprise, though, may have been the bathroom; mine is filled with built-ins, and I'm betting yours is as well. Cabinetry is essential in this space, organizing everything from makeup to first aid essentials, while sinks and vanities are often built in, too. Likewise, a linen closet, tub, and shower—even the wall niche that holds soaps and shampoos—are built-ins essential to everyday living.

The point is this: The possibilities for built-ins are at every turn. In entries, hallways, and stairways. Throughout workspaces and craft rooms. Even in the laundry room. If writing this book has done nothing else it's made me realize how many built-ins I count on daily, and how many more I'd like to update or add to my home. I've already started my priority list. I have a feeling, after reading this book, you'll be doing the same.

why built-ins?

●●●

THE WORD *BUILT-INS* IMMEDIATELY CONJURES UP MENTAL IMAGES OF bookshelves and cabinetry throughout the house. In fact, their possibilities are much more far-reaching. In a mudroom, a mere sliver of space might be devoted to built-in seating, the perfect spot to pull on boots or change shoes. Likewise, built-in bunk beds can be a good solution in a child's room, whether it's shared on a regular basis or always ready for sleepovers.

Built-ins can also be one of the best ways to customize your home, to define your own style and shape your space. Whether you're building a new residence or remodeling your current one, they can reflect your sense of personal style as much as the clothes you wear; it's all in the details. Plus built-ins are adept at defining and shaping spaces. In a great room, for instance, an island can visually separate the kitchen from the adjacent family room.

The beauty of built-ins lies in the fact that they allow you to create storage and display space practically anywhere. What's more, you can make the most of every square inch, a real benefit if you have limited space. Built-in storage that reaches from floor to ceiling can offer twice the space—or more— than a piece of freestanding furniture with the same footprint.

Built-in display shelves turn what could have been a neglected space between the living room and stairway into a treat for the eye. Because they reach to the ceiling, the shelves also make the space appear taller.

Last but not least, comfort should be as much of a priority as style and sensibility. Add built-ins that increase the livability of your home and make everyday tasks easier. You'll quickly find that the monetary investment will be returned many times over.

define style and shape space

●●● IT STANDS TO REASON THAT BUILT-INS should complement the rest of your home. Down to the last detail, they should of course blend seamlessly in terms of style, but color, size, and configuration need to be harmonious, too. That's easy to accomplish if built-ins are incorporated during the building process, but units added as part of a remodeling should look original to the residence as well.

In addition to reinforcing a certain style, built-ins can shape a room's space. Strategically placed cabinets, islands—even seating—can carve a great room into more intimate areas, adding architectural appeal in the process. Likewise, floor-to-ceiling shelves can create walls, perhaps dividing a single space into separate living and dining areas; if the storage is accessible from both sides, so much the better. Even a built-in half wall can create a visual divider and, fitted with cabinets or shelves, serve up storage too.

FACING PAGE TOP LEFT While a frameless shower would have shaped the space in this master bath, this built-in shower—faced in pale blue tile and reaching the ceiling—makes a stronger statement.

FACING PAGE BOTTOM This kitchen would have had a completely different personality without the turquoise-painted island. Had it matched the rest of the white cabinetry, the room's mood would have been much more subdued.

ABOVE Built-ins get much of the credit for this smart-looking family room; display shelves flanking the fireplace plus a nearby entertainment cabinet are as functional as they are chic. An inviting window seat provides an extra level of comfort.

BELOW This kitchen's built-ins define its style and shape its space. Streamlined cabinetry establishes a certain contemporary ambiance, while the combination island/breakfast bar defines the kitchen's boundaries.

create storage and display areas

●●● BUILT-IN CABINETS ARE A GIVEN IN ANY kitchen; they're essential to making the space functional. Kitchen islands too are often built in; their sturdy presence can multiply the amount of storage space, especially if all four sides are used. But there are opportunities for built-in cabinets and closets throughout the house. In a mudroom, for example, locker-style storage is well suited for everything from coats and hats to sports gear. And there's perhaps nothing more luxurious than a perfectly appointed master closet, outfitted not only with the requisite rods but also with shoe racks and drawers designed for specific purposes.

Shelves, though, are perhaps the most versatile of all built-ins. They can serve a purely utilitarian purpose in the pantry or offer display space for decorative objects in the living room. In fact, built-in shelves and their contents provide the opportunity to infuse a room with your personality; whether it's art objects or collectibles, family photos or books, they all speak to your individuality.

RIGHT The scalloped trim and ornamental hardware on this built-in storage piece make it a good fit for the country-chic room, but it's the wallpapered back that takes the decorative expression to an even higher level.

RIGHT In this master bath, lower shelves keep towels close at hand while the upper shelves are reserved for treasured collectibles, giving what could have been a sterile space a spark of personality.

ABOVE Built-ins on either side of the fireplace create workspaces with storage drawers as well as upper shelves that are handy for both work essentials and items purely for display.

LEFT Stacked wall cabinets reach all the way to the ceiling in this kitchen, making it seem taller in the process. The glass-fronted doors of the upper cabinets make it easy to see what's inside; a library-style ladder provides access.

add comfort and charm

● ● ● WHILE BUILT-INS CAN SERVE UTILITARIAN or decorative purposes, they can add an element of comfort too. Upholstered banquette seating might be well suited for a breakfast nook, where the family starts each day together. Or a built-in window seat may provide a welcoming place to escape with a good book—or simply your own thoughts.

But the element of comfort goes beyond the physical aspect; incorporating your personal style can be pleasing to the point of being uplifting. Built-in shelves filled with a treasured collection of art glass might speak to your contemporary preferences. Likewise, built-in bunk beds crafted of reclaimed wood might reveal your country—or eco-friendly—tendencies. Surrounding yourself with things familiar and favorite is what comfort and charm are all about.

ABOVE These built-in bunk beds are framed to share a tall window, so there's no chance of occupants feeling claustrophobic. Storage drawers tucked below the beds provide a convenient place for extra linens.

RIGHT Built-in banquette seating tucks neatly under the windows in this kitchen. Teamed with a table and bench that are just as modern as the upholstery fabric, the banquette is a comfortable spot for a family meal or a quiet cup of coffee.

FACING PAGE A dressing area in this master suite is the epitome of luxury. In addition to built-in clothes storage lining each side of the space, twin window seats—with drawers below—flank the fireplace.

cabinets, drawers, and shelves

● ● ●

ALTHOUGH CABINETS ARE MOST OFTEN ASSOCIATED WITH KITCHENS and bathrooms, their capacity for organization makes them a good fit for any room. In the living room, cabinets can house media equipment; in the dining room, they can keep dinnerware close at hand. Cabinets in a bedroom can provide convenient clothes storage, while in a child's room, they can corral toys.

In addition to being hardworking, cabinets have the ability to set the style of a room. Plus, depending on their size, they can shape a space, affect traffic patterns, and impact your budget. You'll find a vast assortment of stock and semicustom cabinets, or you might opt for custom cabinetry. But consider your timetable. Custom or semicustom cabinets can take time to construct, and even a stock cabinet may not be available to pull immediately from the store's shelf. If you're a do-it-yourselfer, and trying to keep costs down, there are knockdown (KD) and ready-to-assemble (RTA) options. Whichever you choose, educate yourself on door and drawer types as well as cabinet accessories.

Flanking the sink in this laundry room are cabinets and drawers that keep detergents, stain removers, and all manner of essentials close at hand. Meanwhile, wall shelves hold smaller laundry-related items as well as decorative objects.

Cabinets reign supreme in terms of built-in storage, but open shelves have their clear advantages too. The most basic of all built-ins, shelves have endless possibilities and are budget friendly. Short or long, wide or narrow, shelves can be tucked into any room. Give some thought, though, as to what your shelves will hold; those intended for heavy loads such as books, for instance, will need sufficient support.

cabinets

●●● CABINETS ARE DEFINED BY THEIR STYLE and function but all start with nothing more than a basic box, be it face frame or frameless. The more traditional face-frame cabinet gets its style and strength from a frame of horizontal rails and vertical stiles applied to the exposed edges of the case. Doors and drawers mount to that frame, either fitting flush or overlaying all or part of it. Because it takes more time to construct components that must fit closely together, face-frame cabinets with inset doors and drawers are pricier than those with overlays.

As its name implies, a frameless cabinet—often referred to as European-style—is a box with no face frame; its streamlined appearance is well suited for modern or contemporary rooms. Because there's no frame to add stability, the case itself must be built stronger than its face-frame counterpart; ¾-in.-thick sides make the sturdiest frameless case. At first glance, it's not always easy to distinguish face-frame cabinets from frameless; doors and drawers for both can be flush overlay.

ABOVE These traditional-style face-frame cabinets with inset doors and drawers are crafted in rich walnut. Appropriately, they're topped with crown molding although—in a twist—accented with contemporary hardware.

RIGHT In this kitchen, the face-frame cabinetry with overlay doors and drawers takes on a country quality. Base cabinets are fronted with classic beadboard and all hardware is in the same country vein; even the glass-fronted upper cabinets reveal a penchant for the style.

FACE-FRAME VS. FRAMELESS CABINETS: WHAT'S THE DIFFERENCE?

THE CABINET CASE

- A **face-frame** cabinet can make it easier to fit cabinets into a space that isn't completely square and plumb.
- A **face-frame** cabinet has a narrower opening than a **frameless** cabinet of the same width, so pull-out shelves and drawers must be narrower too.
- A **frameless** cabinet has no stile or rail in front of the contents, so it can be easier to pull out stored items; an exception is an especially wide cabinet, which may require a center post.
- A **face-frame** cabinet gets much of its strength from the frame, whereas a **frameless** cabinet depends on a stronger, thicker back and strong corner joints.

DOORS AND DRAWERS

- In **frameless** cabinets, doors and drawers usually overlay the case completely (referred to as full overlay or flush overlay). Frameless cabinets rarely have inset doors.
- In **face-frame** cabinets, doors and drawers may overlay the frame completely, may be inset, or may overlay the frame partially (referred to as reveal overlay or half overlay).
- Inset doors require more precision in their construction and installation than overlay doors.

DOOR HARDWARE

- Concealed adjustable hinges are available for both **frameless** and **face-frame** cabinet doors. They commonly adjust in three directions and are easy to tweak over the lifetime of a cabinet.
- Inset doors are typically hung with butt hinges, which require more precision to install than their adjustable counterparts.

CABINET SHELVES

- Fixed or adjustable shelves can be a less expensive option than pull-out shelves in both **frameless** and **face-frame** cabinets because pull-out shelves require slide hardware.
- Pull-out shelves offer easier overall access to contents than do fixed or adjustable shelves.

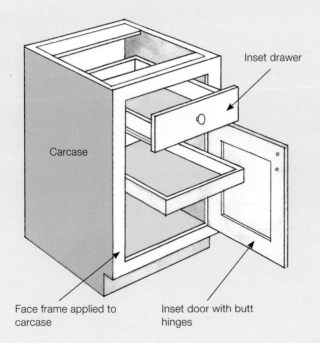

FACE-FRAME CABINET

Inset drawer

Carcase

Face frame applied to carcase

Inset door with butt hinges

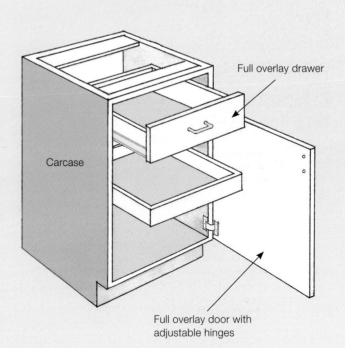

FRAMELESS CABINET

Full overlay drawer

Carcase

Full overlay door with adjustable hinges

Although face-frame cabinetry is the most traditional type, this example proves it can take on a contemporary flair. Inset doors and drawers are accented with modern hardware, while frosted-glass doors on the top cabinets further emphasize the style.

A mix of cabinets and open shelves adds to the visual appeal of this kitchen. The face-frame cabinetry has, for the most part, solid doors, although a single glass-fronted door exposes colorful dishes. Open shelves are primarily reserved for cookbooks and favorite tea sets.

more about...
CABINET MATERIALS

When it comes to cabinets, beauty is more than skin deep; it's important to look beyond stylish doors and drawers to see what your cabinets are made of. Most are made of wood—whether solid or veneered onto cabinet cases, doors, and drawers—and offered in a wide variety of wood species and finishes. There are mixed opinions as to what type of cabinet case is ideal, but if you live in a moist climate, solid wood may not be your best bet; instead, consider wood veneered onto a more stable material, such as high-quality **plywood**. Many believe that the highest quality wood cabinet cases are made from ¾-in. veneer-core plywood, which is stronger, lighter weight, and more moisture resistant than medium-density fiberboard (**MDF**) or **particleboard**. On the other hand, some cabinetmakers prefer MDF to plywood for its dimensional stability and its smooth face, ideal for applying veneers and other laminates. Plus it's typically less expensive than veneer-core plywood. Finally, while particleboard is inarguably the

lowest-quality case good material, it's also the least expensive and, as a result, the most commonly used in manufactured cabinets. If your budget allows, choose plywood for cabinets in areas where water damage could potentially occur. For dry locations, look to MDF or even particleboard but also consider a plywood mash up, combination core panels; its strong and light veneer plywood core is sandwiched between layers of MDF to provide a smooth, stable surface.

If chemical sensitivity is a concern, know that plywood, MDF, and particleboard are all more green than in the past; they emit less formaldehyde thanks to improved glues. But while formaldehyde levels are very low in all three products, there are slight differences among them. Veneer-core plywood contains the least formaldehyde, whereas MDF has more than particleboard. Finally, look for cabinets tagged with "no added formaldehyde" or consider pricier, all-metal cabinets.

European-style cabinetry in this streamlined space is in keeping with the kitchen's sleek design. The color scheme is understated, save for the plum-colored glass backsplash.

•configuring cabinetry

All cabinets are not created equal; their size and shape can vary greatly depending on their intended use. (See individual chapters for specific room recommendations.) Custom or semicustom cabinets can be built to your preferred heights and depths. If you're particularly handy, you might even be able to retrofit KD or RTA cabinets.

As diverse as cabinets can be, however, they also have their similarities. Kitchen and bath cabinets, for instance, typically feature toe spaces (or toekicks) that allow you to stand close to the counter. Created by the recessed frame that supports the cabinet—or from trim that conceals cabinet support legs—a standard toe space is 4 in. high and 3 in. deep, but the toe space of a European-style cabinet is more often 5 in. to 8 in. high. The higher toe space creates a more generous place to stand and makes it easier to reach items in upper wall cabinets. Plus a higher toe space allows additional room to install a built-in step stool or heat and return-air registers.

Unfitted-style cabinetry features a dark-painted toe space flanked with legs that have the look of furniture. Conversely, some kitchen and bath cabinets are set on plinths that project from the case; while this makes for a truly traditional look, it also requires a countertop with a deep overhang to allow room for your feet. If plinth-based cabinets are in other areas of the house, though—where you'll not be standing to work at a countertop—the extended base is not an issue.

For cabinetry to truly have a built-in look, continue the exact style and height of your wall's baseboard around the cabinets. On the other hand, if you want your built-in to look like a piece of furniture, consider a base different in shape and size from the wall's baseboard.

FACING PAGE TOP A mix of wood and white-painted cabinetry complement each other in this kitchen. The clean look is magnified by the absence of wall cabinets; instead, open shelves between the room's windows keep everyday items within easy reach.

FACING PAGE BOTTOM Wood or white cabinetry is often the norm but that doesn't mean you have to rule out other colors. Base cabinets in this butler's pantry are lacquered a deep blue, giving them more importance—and visual weight—than the white, glass-fronted wall cabinets.

ABOVE In a room with a vaulted ceiling, built-in cabinetry can make the most of what otherwise could have been a hard-to-treat wall. To take this storage unit to its desired height, the top right corner is angled to fit the sloped ceiling.

In the spirit of a true built-in, this unit is trimmed with the same crown molding and baseboard as the surrounding walls. A graphic-patterned wallpaper backs the shelves, carrying out the room's blue-and-white color scheme.

more about...
CABINET SOURCES

Cabinets have a wide range of sources and, contrary to what you may believe, **custom** cabinets aren't necessarily the most expensive. They can be if their fabrication takes longer than semicustom cabinets. But a cabinetmaker may combine components from several specialized sources with shop-built cases, an approach that can result in both a shorter lead time and a better product. What's more, it can be a less-expensive alternative to higher-end semicustom cabinetry.

Stock and semicustom cabinets typically come from cabinet manufacturers that purchase parts from companies specializing in doors, drawers, or cases. **Stock** cabinets can be purchased right off the shelf or ordered from a big-box store, home center, or lumberyard or through a kitchen designer or contractor. (Installation is generally available for an additional fee.) Stock cabinets are typically built in standard-size components in 3-in. increments, and if a run of cabinets isn't quite as wide as you

need, there are filler pieces that can span the gaps. Available in a wide array of styles and sizes, colors and finishes, stock cabinets typically run about half the cost of semicustom and custom cabinets.

Semicustom cabinets are also manufactured (as opposed to shopmade) and are made to order for a specific project; cabinets can be built as larger assemblies rather than simply case by case. Available in a wider range of styles, finishes, sizes, and configurations than stock cabinets, and with more hardware and accessory options, semicustom cabinetry tends to be higher quality and higher priced than stock cabinets, sometimes by a considerable amount.

Don't hesitate to mix and match cabinet types; you might opt for custom or semicustom cabinets for high-visibility locations, such as a kitchen island, and use stock or DIY (KD or RTA) cabinets around the room's perimeter.

ABOVE The charcoal-gray cabinetry in this kitchen blends quietly into a backdrop of nearly matching subway tiles. Although the dark neutrals could have made the room feel closed in, the absence of wall cabinets—shelves are used instead—and linear windows open up the room.

LEFT Full overlay doors and drawers get much of the credit for this kitchen's clean-lined look, which is further enhanced by the cabinetry's frame-and-flat-panel fronts. At the same time, their straightforward design allows the mullioned wall cabinets to take star status.

•choosing doors and drawers

Doors and drawers present the best opportunity to make your cabinetry as understated or as elaborate as you like. The simplest style is a flat slab, while frame-and-panel doors can be clean lined or complex; the panels can be flat, raised, or made of beadboard or fitted with clear, frosted, or textured glass.

When making decisions on door and drawer faces, keep in mind that inset doors and drawers, which fit flush with a face frame, tend to be more costly than overlay doors because of the extra precision required to build them. You'll find that hinges on inset cabinets are visible, with mortised butt hinges and leaf hinges being the most traditional styles.

Overlay doors and drawers affix to the surface of a face frame or the interior of a frameless case, and cup hinges make them easily adjustable. Full overlay doors and drawers, the standard on frameless cabinets but also used on face-frame cabinets, all but touch each other. Thus they're more painstaking to build and install than reveal-overlay doors and drawers, which are spaced farther apart. Reveal-overlay doors and drawers, also referred to as partial overlay, are used on face-frame cabinets.

Mirrored cabinet doors not only add a touch of elegance but also make a small space seem larger. In a room that's traditional in style, antiqued mirror can add an old-fashioned look.

Proof that cabinetry need not be symmetrical, the wall cabinets to the left of this cooktop feature a conventional mix of solid and glass-fronted doors, while to the right, glass-fronted cabinets reach from the countertop to the ceiling, making a dramatic impact.

BASE CABINETS:
DRAWER FACE AND DOOR OPTIONS

t here are two basic categories of drawers and doors: frame and panel and flat slab. Some cabinet cases shown here are frameless and others are face frame, but either category of doors and drawers can be used in either type of cabinet. Although door and drawer faces should be compatible, they don't need to be identical. Keep in mind that detailing on shallow drawers looks best if it's simpler than that on a door or wide drawer.

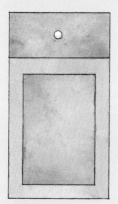

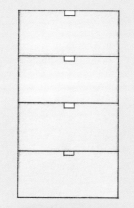

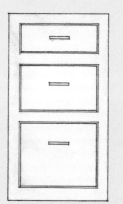

Flat-slab drawer over a frame-and-panel door with concealed hinges

A shallow drawer often looks less fussy with a flat-slab face, plus it pairs well with any kind of door.

Drawer in a beaded-edge frame over a beaded frame-and-raised-panel door with butt hinges

The drawer face echoes the beading detail on the door design but doesn't go so far as to repeat the raised panel.

A stack of same-size flat-slab overlay drawers with finger pulls

The clean-lined overlay drawers have a contemporary look, enhanced by the streamlined hardware.

Graduated drawers in a beaded face-frame case with intermediate rails

Intermediate rails provide strength and a traditional look. Beading the frame instead of the drawer also offers a simpler detail that will withstand the test of time.

Graduated drawers in a face-frame cabinet without intermediate rails

Eliminating the intermediate rails between drawers has a less traditional look but provides more cabinet capacity.

European-style cabinets fill every inch of this U-shaped kitchen, their characteristic flat-slab doors creating a streamlined look. The outer leg of the U features cabinets on both sides, doubling as a divider between the kitchen and the adjacent living area.

ABOVE This kitchen is high on textural appeal, evident in the built-in island. European-style cabinetry in a smooth, white-lacquer finish is flanked by rough-hewn brick—also in white—and topped with a butcher-block countertop.

RIGHT A two-tier drawer like the one under this wall oven and warming drawer is deep enough—and strong enough—to hold a wide variety of frequently used pots and pans.

Lazy Susans are one way to make the most of corner cabinetry, but corner drawers like these are another great use of space. They can be the better option when you want to keep small, often-used items close to the countertop.

Incorporating elements of universal design is a smart strategy for any kitchen. These slide-out drawers give a clear view of pots and pans, and make them more easily accessible.

DRAWER DETAILS

oday's drawers do some heavy lifting, so be sure that yours are up to the task. In the kitchen, they'll be supporting pots and pans as well as stacks of dishes; in the home office, they're apt to hold heavy file folders. Look for drawer boxes built with ⅝-in. to ¾-in. melamine, solid wood, or birch plywood. Shallow drawers, on the other hand, may have side panels as thin as ½ in. Metal and plastic sides typically have sufficient strength, too, and have a more streamlined look. Finally, keep in mind that shelves that carry particularly heavy loads should be thick.

Drawers are operated by glides, also referred to as guides or slides. Full-extension glides allow access to the entire length of a drawer, a convenience that may well be worth the extra expense. Or you might want to opt for quiet, self-closing glides. Most glides are side mounted, but if you don't like the look, undermounts are another option. Keep in mind, however, that they are more expensive than side-mounted glides and can be used only on face-frame cabinets. Undermount glides reduce the depth of the drawer, whereas side-mounted glides shave a bit off the width.

For the most part, hardware is a matter of personal preference. But a wide drawer—one that measures 24 in. or more—requires two knobs, two short pulls, or one long pull. When choosing knobs and pulls, keep proportion in mind. A 1¼-in. knob, for instance, is a good size for a standard-size drawer. A knob with a rose (the round plate at the base of the shaft) can keep things neater, simply because fingers are less likely to touch the drawer itself. By the same token, bin pulls have a cleaner look because they're grabbed from the inside; on the downside, however, they are a little more difficult to clean than knobs.

drawers vs. pull-out shelves

In base cabinets, drawers have their advantages but so do pull-out shelves. With low sides and fronts, pull-out shelves allow a quick inventory of their contents. On the other hand, because their walls aren't as high as those of a drawer, items can fall out; a drawer is better at corralling its contents. Another advantage of a drawer is that it takes just one motion to see what's inside. With a pull-out shelf, you first have to open a cabinet door and then tug on the shelf. (There are base cabinets, however, that feature a stack of pull-out shelves attached directly to the cabinet door panel that glides straight out with one motion.) Finally, you may want to consider cost: An all-drawer base cabinet is more expensive than one with a drawer on top and a door concealing pull-out shelves on the bottom.

ABOVE More than the standard cutlery drawer, this one is customized to suit specific needs and incorporates a sliding compartment at the top to provide easy access to items at the back.

RIGHT When closed, this cabinet appears to be three graduated drawers. In fact, though, the top drawer is conventionally outfitted for flatware while the bottom portion is outfitted with canisters to hold utensils.

LEFT Because dishes can get heavy, they're well suited to base cabinet drawers. Plus they're easier to access than if they're in wall cabinets. This drawer is custom fitted with wooden dowels to keep the stacks of dishes from touching one another.

LEFT What could easily have been a neglected corner is devoted to an appliance garage that houses the toaster. A fold-back door and pull-out shelf make for easy access.

A single cabinet in this kitchen pulls out to reveal three tiers, each one deeper than the last. In addition, the cabinet face is in keeping with the room's clean look.

A pair of pull-out shelves beneath this cooktop keeps a wide variety of pots and pans conveniently close. The open shelves also allow you to see at a glance what's there—and what's not.

shelves

●●● WHETHER SHORT OR TALL, WIDE OR narrow, open shelves can be an asset in any room of the house. What's more, they're easily accessible. Spice jars in the kitchen and books in the study are good candidates for shelves, as are baskets filled with pint-size toys in a child's room. Open shelves can also be the perfect place to display treasured collectibles. They are cost-effective and there's one more advantage: The visibility of their contents provides incentive to keep things tidy.

As a rule of thumb for storing frequently used items, the shelf should be just slightly deeper than the objects themselves. That way, there's less likelihood that you'll place more items along the shelf's front edge. In a pantry, for instance, wrap three walls with narrow C-shaped shelves or two walls with L-shaped shelves; the narrower shelves will provide easier access and better visibility. Deep shelves, on the other hand, are best for decorative objects, items that you won't need to retrieve on a regular basis.

When it comes to bookshelves, there are some general height guidelines: 10½ in. for most books, 12 in. for magazines in stand-up storage boxes, and 13 in. to 14 in. for large art books and oversize cookbooks. Recommended depths for bookshelves are typically between 8 in. and 12 in.

FACING PAGE LEFT To the left of the fireplace in this living room, a combination of cabinets and shelves creates an efficient work area. The built-in desk has just enough work surface to accommodate a tablet, a keyboard, and a few other essentials, while shelves above keep books within easy reach.

FACING PAGE RIGHT Ash-gray base cabinets and shelves make a dramatic statement against a marble backdrop in this kitchen. The shelves are uninterrupted by the window, allowing more storage space and plenty of natural light, too.

ABOVE Shelves echo the angles of this vaulted ceiling, giving the architecture more emphasis in the process. The lower shelves are reserved for oft-used items while those above are primarily for display.

Beyond serving its intended purpose as a library, recessed cabinetry in this living room has aesthetic value. The built-ins' tall height and deep chocolate-brown color visually balance the fireplace and TV between them.

ABOVE Under-stairs space is often neglected, but in this entry it's put to good use. Graduated shelves are filled with some of the owner's favorite treasures, keeping them in plain sight yet tucked away safely.

TOP RIGHT Taking advantage of every square inch of space, built-in shelves are nestled into one end of this island. It's the ideal place for spice jars and cookbooks—items that can quickly be reached and just as quickly be put away.

BOTTOM RIGHT A combination of cabinets and shelves makes perfect sense in a pantry; shelves provide easy access for everyday staples, and drawers can hold everything from spices to dishes. Small appliances can be housed in base cabinets.

•shelf materials and support

Selecting the best shelf material comes down, in large part, to aesthetics, but with each choice there are unique material qualities to keep in mind. Solid wood is relatively strong, but it can warp. Plus it expands and contracts with changes in the humidity. Veneered plywood, on the other hand, is more stable than solid wood and can pass for solid wood if its edges are covered with an edging or edgeband (which also increases the strength of the shelf). Although MDF and particleboard can't span as far as solid wood or plywood shelves of the same thickness and depth, they're certainly serviceable if their supports are close enough together to prevent sagging.

Here are some ways to strengthen a shelf and effectively increase the load it can carry:
- Keep spans short. An increase in span of just 25% results in twice as much deflection.
- Add a cleat, a narrow board that runs continuously under the back side of a shelf.
- Add a 1½-in. edgeband to the front or just under the front edge of the shelf.
- Double the thickness of the shelf by fastening two boards and finishing the front edge with a band that covers both.
- Add intermediate shelf supports.
- Build a torsion box. This thick shelf is similar to a hollow-core door, with a honeycomb structure or plywood strips faced with two plywood skins.

These boxed shelves take the place of conventional wall cabinets, keeping items within easy reach while still protecting them—to a degree—from dust and kitchen splatters. The corners are easy to access too, not always the case with standard cabinetry.

ABOVE Thick shelves like these are a necessity in the kitchen, where stacks of dishes can be hefty. These carry out the room's linear theme, too, echoing the straight lines of the wood-wrapped island as well as the cabinets' hardware.

RIGHT Intermediate supports allow these shelves to hold more, and heavier, items. It's a particularly good solution here, where foodstuffs are stored in glass containers that can weigh as much, or more, as the staples themselves.

•shelf types

Choosing between fixed and adjustable shelves comes down to their purpose and your personal preference. Fixed shelves are stronger and thus can have longer spans, making them a good choice for open shelves in the kitchen. And because there's no need to drill holes on each side of a cabinet, they have a cleaner look. Adjustable shelves can be a better option in some cases, though; in a child's closet, they can be moved as he or she grows.

This marble shelf, tucked under a bathroom mirror, is just deep enough to hold a razor and other everyday necessities. The shelf material is handsome in its own right but decorative supports further enhance its charm.

more about...
SHELF SUPPORTS

ADJUSTABLE SHELVES

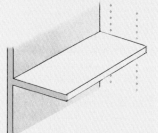

32 mm adjustable shelves

In this common method of supporting shelves, two columns of holes drilled into the sides of cabinets 32 mm apart allow adjustment. Shelf supports vary, from long wire clips that tuck into a groove in shelf ends to clips and pins of various shapes, sizes, and materials. This system suits any type of shelf material.

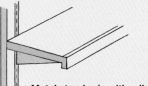

Metal standards with adjustable brackets

To add visual depth and stability, a wood edgeband is applied to the front edge of a shelf. Adjustable brackets mount into slotted standards, though, for a cleaner look, metal standards can be recessed into the wall.

FIXED SHELVES

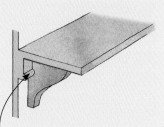

Wood or MDF brackets

Supporting a shelf on a cleat along the back can greatly increase the load that a shelf can support or the distance it can span between brackets or wall supports.

For an extra-thick shelf, apply a same-depth edgeband to a doubled layer of wood or MDF.

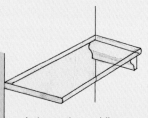

A decorative molding can act as a cleat for solid or glass shelves. A light load and/ or short span may need only supports at each end (shown), while longer spans or heavier loads may require additional support along the back.

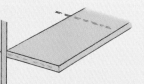

A floating shelf can be supported on hidden rods or bars that are attached to studs. A thick floating shelf may be made of a hollowcore shelf glued to a cleat.

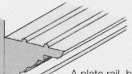

A plate rail, built from stock molding pieces, can be just as functional as it is decorative.

A pair of shelves span this small niche, keeping barware within easy reach. Custom shelves are also built into the adjacent wall; each compartment is big enough to hold a bottle of wine.

While adjustable shelves may seem attractive because they can so easily be moved, in truth, most people never change the positions at all. Fixed shelves have the advantage of being stronger and thus can have longer spans. Plus there's no need to drill holes on each side of a cabinet or bookcase or to install metal standards. If adjustable shelves are necessary—in a child's closet, for instance—consider drilling just a few holes where you need them now and adding more later, once higher shelves are required.

Either fixed or adjustable shelves can be used for books, although fixed shelves are stronger, making them a good choice for a collection of hardbacks. These shelves are symmetrical in their design, creating a formality that's a good fit for this living room.

LEFT A recessed alcove in this kitchen is just a few inches deep but what it lacks in depth it makes up for in height. Both the base and single glass shelf can hold tall items such as oil cans, vinegar bottles, and even decorative pieces.

more about...
RECESSED SHELVES

r ecessed shelves are an option, too, though they should be tucked into interior walls where insulation is not a concern. (The exception may be a particularly thick wall that is deep enough to accommodate both the insulation and a built-in.) A recessed shelf near a cooktop, for instance, can keep spices close at hand; likewise, a recessed shelf in the shower is handy for soaps and shampoos. Before cutting into any existing wall, though, make exploratory holes to determine if any utilities are running behind it.

ABOVE This short wall near a doorway could have been left plain, but instead, recessed shelves showcase some of the owner's treasured collectibles. The same height as the doorway, the shelves draw the eye upward, making the room seem taller in the process.

A pair of deep shelves makes perfect sense in this laundry room; each is large enough to accommodate a basket full of clean clothes. Floor space below is reserved for the family pet, and a simple curtain can be pulled over the entire area.

seating

● ● ●

MUCH OF THE BEAUTY OF BUILT-IN SEATING IS THAT IT MAKES THE
most of every square inch. A breakfast nook, for instance, might be tucked into
a niche where a table and four chairs wouldn't fit. Likewise, an otherwise unused
window bay can be converted into a cozy place to read and relax. What's more,
built-in seating can help shape a room's sense of style. A breakfast booth—with all
the charm of a 1950s-style diner—or a high-backed bench in a mudroom can serve
as strong focal points in their own right.

Where built-in seating is located can make a difference in its design, too. A bench
inside the back door doesn't need an overhanging lip (as is recommended, for
comfort reasons, in eating areas); you're not likely to sit there for more than a few
minutes—just long enough to put on or take off boots. By the same token, a back-
entry bench doesn't need to be topped with a cushion, so you can incorporate
storage under a lift-up seat, if you like. Size and scale come into play as well. In a
living room, you may want to create a cozy nook for one. But if your built-in seating
is intended to take the place of a conventional sofa, it will
need to be just as wide and deep.

**Banquette seating
tucked under a
window teams up with
a glass-top table in
this kitchen. The teal
upholstery makes it a
comfy spot for a casual
meal or to work on
homework. Because
the table is easy to
move, the built-in
drawers are readily
accessible.**

seating to suit every space

●●● ALTHOUGH BREAKFAST NOOKS, WINDOW seats—even mudroom benches—may be the first types of built-in seating that come to mind, there are plenty of other opportunities throughout the house. In a study, built-in seating between two bookcases all but begs you to snuggle down and read. In a child's room, a built-in bench might be designed to double as a toy box. Even in a bathroom, a built-in bench can introduce an element of spa-like comfort. Positioned near the tub or shower, it can offer a slip-free place to dry off (adding a measure of safety, too). But if it's not in a wet area, it might be upholstered, upping the ante of the room's style. The bottom line is this: The possibilities are all around you.

A square-cornered, U-shaped bench might have been the conventional approach to seating just inside this home's entry. Instead, a pair of matching seats features soft curves, echoing the shape of the impressive window.

built-in seating presents a great opportunity for extra storage. A hinged top, for instance, allows you to stash large or seasonal items, even extra blankets and pillows. If, however, there are small children in the house, it's important that the bins are lockable; otherwise, kids could slam the lids on their small fingers or be tempted to climb inside during a game of hide-and-seek. As an alternative, consider fitting a built-in seat with drawers that can be accessed from the front or—in the case of an eating booth—from the ends.

ABOVE Located near the home's entry, but adjacent to a living area, this built-in functions as a coat rack, with storage above and below for small items, as well as an inviting sitting spot.

RIGHT An L-shaped banquette defines this kitchen's casual eating area, the blue-patterned upholstery emphasizing its importance in a room full of otherwise solid colors. The base of this built-in is set back from the seat, allowing occupants to tuck their feet under.

•built-in dining

There's something warm and welcoming about built-in dining. Whether it's a casual breakfast nook or more formal banquette seating, built-in dining can be configured like a booth—with two benches facing one another—or with benches in an L or U shape. For booth-style and U-shaped seating, it's important to choose a pedestal table that won't interfere with diners getting in and out (booth-style seating also allows you to attach the table to the wall for greater stability). On the other hand, a four-legged table can be used with L-shaped seating but make sure it's lightweight, so it can be easily moved for cleaning. There's something to be said as well for using a combination of built-in and chair seating around a freestanding table, especially one with leaves that can accommodate additional guests or a wheelchair.

ABOVE Banquettes are commonplace in kitchens, but that doesn't mean they can't be at home in formal dining rooms. This cream-colored banquette is elegantly understated with complementary chairs and a pedestal table to help set the mood.

LEFT Making the most of every square inch of this niche, U-shaped built-in seating teams up with a wood table and a pair of freestanding chairs. The back of the banquette is angled just enough to add an extra element of comfort.

BUILT-IN COMFORT

because friends and family often congregate in the kitchen, it's important to incorporate comfy seating. With a little thought and planning, a built-in eating area can be as appealing as your favorite easy chair.

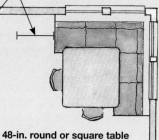

Bumped out, stepped up, and surrounded by windows, this breakfast nook feels like a room of its own. Drawer storage is built into each end of the bench; one or both drawers might be set up as charging stations, especially if the nook doubles as a homework spot.

THE TRADITIONAL BREAKFAST BOOTH

A breakfast nook with benches requires a pedestal or trestle table, or—in a two-sided booth like this—the wall on one end and a central leg near the other can support the table. For bench length, figure on about 24 in. per adult for comfort.

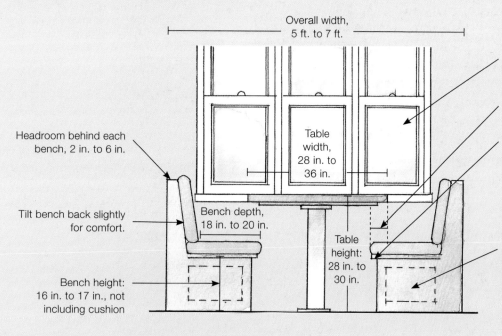

Overall width, 5 ft. to 7 ft.

Headroom behind each bench, 2 in. to 6 in.

Tilt bench back slightly for comfort.

Bench height: 16 in. to 17 in., not including cushion

Bench depth, 18 in. to 20 in.

Table width, 28 in. to 36 in.

Table height: 28 in. to 30 in.

Keep the window as low as possible, even lower than the tabletop if you like.

Table/bench overlap: 4 in. to 5 in.

Bench overhang: 2 in. to 4 in. An overhang makes it more comfortable for your legs. Allow the cushion to overhang the bench for back-of-the-knee comfort.

Benches have potential for storage underneath, but it will be difficult to access bench-top storage, especially if the table is built-in. Drawers or shelves in the bench end are easier to use.

OTHER WAYS TO CONFIGURE BUILT-IN DINING

Allow at least 32 in. to 36 in. between any wall cabinet and the end of the bench/edge of table.

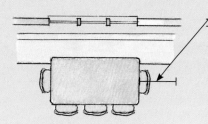

36-in. by 72-in. table with a bench on three sides

More bench seating allows for more occupants, especially kids.

36-in. by 72-in. table with a single straight bench

This configuration is more flexible but may not accommodate as many diners as a three-sided bench.

48-in. round or square table with a corner bench

This configuration is both cozy and flexible. Either a round or square table fits beautifully into an angled corner.

•built-in benches

Built-in benches in a breakfast nook can be as comfortable as any chair, especially if they're cushioned or upholstered. Still, it's important that they're positioned at just the right height from the floor and that they have a slight back angle. (See recommendations in "Built-In Comfort" on p. 43.) Your feet should touch the floor, and the front edge of the seat shouldn't cut into your knees. In fact, seats should overhang the bench front—if there is one—a few inches so that your legs have room to move.

Benches are by no means reserved for breakfast nooks, though. In a hallway, a bench might underscore a bank of windows, making the space more of a destination to enjoy the view than a mere passageway. Likewise, a bench located in the kitchen—near, but not in, the main work zone—allows family and friends to converse with the cook.

ABOVE In lieu of a conventional furniture arrangement in this sunroom, built-in sofas at right angles can seat a crowd. Because the seat cushions are the size of twin beds, they can double as overnight accommodations, with linens stored in the drawers below.

LEFT A simple L-shaped bench runs the length of the windows in this living area, providing not only supplementary seating but also easily accessible storage space.

Taking advantage of the corner-turning stairway, a bench is tucked just inside the main entrance of this residence. Like mudrooms, front entries are enhanced by a place to sit and change shoes, and this one offers the bonus of drawer storage for hats, gloves, and mittens.

•built-in window seats

Window seats are often thought of as nooks to curl up in, to read, or to watch the world go by. In fact, though, a window seat can have many functions. In the living room, it can provide extra seating; its built-in aspect can make the most of a room's dimensions, a real advantage in smaller spaces. A window seat can also provide a comfy place to nap, or even serve as a bed for guests. If the seat is 18 in. high, including the cushion, it will be comfortable for all these activities.

To thoroughly appreciate the outdoor view, you'll want to be able to sit sideways. If possible, provide 15-in.-tall backs on each side to lean against, sloped for an extra measure of comfort. If built-in backs are not an option—you might have windows on all three sides, for instance—loose pillows or cushions can add comfort.

ABOVE It takes no more than a sliver of space to create a welcoming window seat. The area at the end of hallways or in bedroom dormers can be a particularly good candidate.

FACING PAGE TOP Trimmed—right down to the baseboard—to exactly match the adjacent storage unit, this built-in window seat is especially inviting, thanks to a thick cushion and throw pillows. The cushion is light enough that storage under the lift-up top is easy to access.

FACING PAGE BOTTOM Niches created by bay and bow windows are natural spots for built-in dining areas. Their angles and curves welcome designs in which diners face each other, perfect for comfortable conversation.

RIGHT It's a plus to have a place where guests can sit and chat with the cook. Running the length of one wall, and tucked under the windows, this upholstered built-in bench features drawer storage, too.

window seats: to bump out or not?

Many window seats are designed to fit into bump-outs in exterior walls. Another option is to fit a window seat between interior walls.

LEFT Set into the bump-out of an exterior wall, this window seat is an appealing place to curl up with a good book or stretch out for an afternoon nap. As a rule, a window seat should be 15 in. to 16 in. high, assuming a 3-in. to 4-in. cushion will top it.

FACING PAGE TOP LEFT If bumping out a wall isn't possible, or even desirable, consider tucking a window seat between interior walls. This one takes advantage of short corner-turning walls on each end as well as tall built-in cabinets.

FACING PAGE TOP RIGHT A window seat just big enough for one fits between cabinets in this country-style kitchen. This perfect place to sit down with a cup of coffee was created simply by topping a deep bin with a thick seat cushion.

FACING PAGE BOTTOM Nestled between two towering built-in cabinets in this breakfast room, a window seat provides cozy seating. Because the table and chairs can be easily moved, the drawers beneath the seat are readily accessible.

entryways, hallways, and stairways

● ● ●

AN ENTRYWAY OFFERS THE FIRST INTRODUCTION TO YOUR HOME, giving guests a clue as to your personal style. Front entryways often take a formal tack, while back entryways are more casual. Both, however, have more than aesthetic value; they also accommodate everyday comings and goings. To that end, built-ins get much of the credit. Inside the front door, for instance, a simple bench may be all that's needed, offering a place to sit down and change shoes. The back entryway, though, is apt to be more of a workhorse. From walls lined with strategically placed shelves, pegs, and hooks to a lineup of locker-style storage—one for each member of the house—the right built-ins can make it easier to get out the door each morning on the way to work or school.

It's not just the entryway that can benefit from built-ins; hallways and stairways can be enhanced with cabinets, shelves, and seating, too. A hallway can be elevated from a mere pass-through by widening it 1 ft. or 2 ft., making room for additional storage. A stairway also provides plenty of opportunities to carve out storage space. Shelves might be built into a stair's landing to display treasured collectibles or the space below a set of stairs can be fitted with doors, drawers, and shelves, making the most of an otherwise unused area.

Making the most of rather limited space, a hardworking wall in this mudroom provides a place to sit down while changing shoes as well as a rack for coats and hats. On either side, built-in shelves hold rattan bins that can corral all manner of small items.

4

entryways

● ● ● A FRONT ENTRYWAY CAN BE JUST AS functional as it is fashionable. With built-in seating, shelving, and a requisite coat closet, it can serve you and your guests well. Even diminutive built-ins can make a big difference in a narrow space; consider a 4-in.-deep shelf at elbow height for keys and sunglasses or a 4-ft.-long peg board for coats.

Unquestionably, though, the back entryway—or mudroom—is more heavily used on a daily basis. It's the drop-off spot for books and backpacks and a place to kick off boots and hang up coats. It can even serve as a wash-up spot and a home to all kinds of sports equipment. To make your mudroom work most efficiently, start by inventorying each family member's needs, then search out the best built-ins to accommodate them. Once your plan is in place, clutter will be a thing of the past.

Mere steps inside the front door, built-in storage differs just enough from the home's architecture that it looks like fine furniture that's been slid into place. What the architecture and built-in have in common, though, is their traditional styling; one is just as elegant as the other.

Just inside the front entrance of this residence, a stairway is defined—and made safer—by a half wall.
But that wall satisfies storage needs, too. Lining the entry hall, individual cubbies hold catch-all baskets, while
built-in bookshelves and drawers face the adjacent living area.

An off-center door in this back entryway
dictated that built-in storage be on one wall.
A cabinet is flanked by matching benches,
each with pull-out storage below. Because the
benches are set back farther than the cabinet,
and all have furniture-like legs, the resulting
look is that of three individual pieces.

Sliding barn-style doors open to reveal storage in this condo's entryway.
On one side, cupboards, hooks, and shelves team up to accommodate coats, shoes,
and the like. On the other, cabinets serve up seasonal storage while providing a
drop-off spot for keys and mail.

ACCOMMODATE YOUR FAMILY'S NEEDS

back entryway built-ins need not be a complex set of cabinets. In fact, simple, easy-to-use elements can often be the best choice. If family members come and go on the run, hooks and pegs might be a better option for coats and hats than a full-fledged closet with hangers. By the same token, baskets and open shelves can make for easy storage and retrieval. Here are a few suggestions for entryway built-ins:

- Place hooks or a dedicated basket at elbow-height for commonly misplaced items like keys and sunglasses.
- By the back door, devote a basket to outgoing mail and library books.
- Build in charging stations for electronics, either a centrally located strip of outlets or outlets in individual lockers.
- Provide enough hooks for in-season coats, jackets, scarves, and hats.
- Supply wall hooks for backpacks or, if each family member has his or her own locker, benches or shelves on which to set them.
- Designate a place for in-season sports gear.
- Provide a place for wet boots.
- To comfortably put on and take off shoes, build in a bench, which can double as storage with doors or drawers below.
- Don't forget about the four-legged members of the family; provide storage space for leashes, kennels, and bowls.

TOP RIGHT Built-in cabinets in this mudroom are topped with a solid surface that reaches down to create a tub for the family dog. One of the cabinets features standard door and drawer storage; the other was left open to create space for a comfy dog bed.

BOTTOM RIGHT Built-in storage is shared with the family pets in this mudroom. Open shelving houses bins for gloves and scarves as well as dog toys; coat hooks provide a space for dog leashes. The stroke of brilliance, though, is in the built-in food and water bowls, including the dedicated faucet.

LEFT In this mudroom, coat hooks make it easy to retrieve outerwear at a moment's notice, and there's a comfy seat below where you can pull on your boots. Just beyond—in addition to plenty of built-in storage—the laundry area makes it possible to throw dirty clothes in the wash before even entering the living spaces.

BOTTOM LEFT This mudroom accommodates an active family. On one wall, coat hooks line up behind a bench, while, on the opposite wall, cubbies, drawers, and bins keep all kinds of sports equipment organized. To the left of the closet at the far end of the room is a small door that's the model of convenience; it opens to access a stack of firewood.

BOTTOM RIGHT Back entryways can often have a cluttered look, but thanks to closed storage, this one is anything but. On one wall, a built-in takes on the look of a fine cabinet, while a nearby bench is underscored by drawer storage. The high cupboards are perfect for little-used items.

•mudrooms

Mudrooms come in all shapes and sizes but should all have one thing in common: They need to be at least 5 ft. wide, allowing enough room for one person to sit on a bench to put on shoes while leaving sufficient space for another to pass by.

Using everything from the smallest hooks and pegs to cubbies, shelves, and full-fledged lockers, there are plenty of opportunities for built-in storage, too; mudrooms are perfectly suited for housing everything from dog leashes and umbrellas to skateboards and baseball bats.

Because the mudroom is, by nature, close to the garage, be sure to provide a landing space for groceries and packages as well. Larger mudrooms can even accommodate recycling bins, making it convenient to roll them out to the curb.

This mudroom contains the requisite bench, coat hooks, and storage cubbies but also features a sink and counter space—perfect for arranging flowers, setting down groceries and mail, or simply washing up after being outside.

gallery

locker-style storage

There's a reason lockers are so popular with the school set: They can store a multitude of personal belongings in a relatively small space. It makes sense, then, that the locker concept has come home, for students and adults alike.

RIGHT These open lockers have the advantage of easy access; even the striped storage baskets above and below can be reached easily. Another built-in benefit is a bench that runs the entire length of the lockers, providing plenty of room to sit down to change shoes.

This set of lockers offers both open and closed storage; the closed versions keep coats under wraps, and their open counterparts allow family members to quickly grab what they need. Beneath the lockers, drawer fronts allow just enough of a view to see what's within.

A mudroom hallway is home to lockers in this residence, the compartmentalized storage keeping coats, hats, and boots—even sports equipment—ready to grab at a moment's notice. Because the lockers are recessed into the wall, they don't take up any valuable pass-through space.

Locker-style storage reaches to the ceiling in this mudroom, the closed cabinetry keeping items neatly out of sight. There's open space beneath each locker too, leaving room for family members' shoes and boots.

•sitting spots

A place to sit is a necessity, especially in a mudroom, where changing shoes and boots is a common occurrence. A freestanding bench could fill the bill, but built-in seating can serve double-duty. The open space below might be used to corral rain boots or other outdoor-only footgear. Alternatively, you might opt for a built-in bench with closed storage below to keep hats, gloves, and mittens close at hand. Closed storage can have a tidier look but, because outerwear requires ventilation in almost any climate, be sure to provide some form of air circulation in closed cubbies or footlockers. Keep in mind, too, that if the wall behind the bench is outfitted with hooks for coats and backpacks, the seating surface should be 2 ft. deep, so you can sit without disturbing the hanging items.

ABOVE When a sitting spot is backed by a series of coat hooks, the seat should be 2 ft. deep so whatever's hanging from above won't brush against occupants. Because this bench is recessed and there's cabinetry overhead, there's a cozy feeling, too.

LEFT A built-in bench in this mudroom takes a simple approach; it's made up of nothing more than an upholstered seat with open shelving below. The shelves were custom built to accommodate rattan baskets, which are easy to pull out.

Lockers in this mudroom have an abbreviated form. Instead of the conventional design—with lockers separated from top to bottom—these have partial dividers, allowing the bench beneath to run the entire length of the built-in storage space.

hallways

●●● HALLWAYS HAVE THE POTENTIAL TO BE so much more than mere passageways. In fact, they can be just as hardworking as any room in the house. Floor-to-ceiling bookshelves can lend a library look, and display shelves allow passers-by to get a good view of your treasures. Small display areas can even be carved out from between studs.

If you've yet to build your dream home, consider widening a main hallway, even by a foot or two. That additional space can be just enough to fit in a built-in bench, a set of shelves, or even a cantilevered work surface that's just big enough for a laptop, making the hallway a destination in its own right as a reading nook or handy home office.

A dead-end hallway all too often goes neglected but that's not the case here. A single piece of wood, cantilevered from the wall, is just large enough to hold a laptop and clip-on light. While the desktop is simple, the accompanying chair is sculptural, its Z-shape eye-catching in its own right.

ABOVE A long hallway can sometimes seem tunnel-like, but this one, lined on both sides with bookshelves, is transformed into a personal library. Shelves reach from floor to ceiling on one side, and the shorter configuration on the other side creates a display shelf.

ABOVE In a hallway with ample room to walk through, built-ins can make an efficient use of space. In this second-floor hallway, a bench is centered on the facing window, taking advantage of the view. It's the surrounding combination of cabinets and shelves, though, that truly make this space effective.

RIGHT The clean lines of these built-in closets are right in step with the contemporary styling of the home. In fact, the only clue that this is anything but a solid wall lies in the streamlined door pulls.

RIGHT With built-in china cupboards flanking the window, this back hallway is a hardworking space. Design continuity is provided by the bench between them, its wooden seat matching the tops of the base cabinets.

ABOVE Built-in storage takes advantage of every inch in this upstairs hallway. Along one wall, closed storage holds everything from bed linens to off-season clothing. There's even more storage space in the adjacent cabinets, coupled with open shelves that display books and favorite finds.

RIGHT In this traditional home, a built-in desk with the same sense of style nestles into one end of a hallway. The workspace itself has the look of a conventional desk but has bonus storage space in ceiling-reaching wall cabinets.

Given that slim computers and laptops are now the norm, a work area can be created in a mere sliver of space. This one tucks between tall cabinets, with storage above for office essentials.

stairways

● ● ● STAIRWAYS CAN BE JUST AS FASHIONABLE as they are functional. But their role can go far beyond simply connecting one floor to another. Beneath a stairway's treads there's plenty of potential for built-in storage or display space, whether it's shelves, drawers, a coat closet, or even a compact workspace. Drawers can be built into risers, too, though care should be taken to always close them completely; a drawer left even slightly open can be a tripping hazard. A safer option is to build drawers into the side of the steps.

Another good opportunity for built-ins is the midway point of a switchback staircase. This can be the perfect place for a window seat or, with shelves carved into stud space, a personal library.

This stair landing is dedicated to recessed shelves; it's the perfect place to display treasured books and collectibles, and the shelves' beadboard backing makes the prized items stand out more prominently.

An under-the-stairs space can be a conundrum, but this home takes full advantage of the area. Outfitted with everything needed for a bar, the entertainment area—with built-in cabinetry and recessed shelving—is conveniently close to where guests mix and mingle.

LEFT Stepped display shelves are inspired by the stairs themselves, providing a place to showcase pieces of pottery. To further emphasize the effect, framed photos take the same stair-stepped direction toward the second floor.

BELOW Stair risers to the top bunk in this boy's room are fitted with drawers, their cut-out handles making them easy to access. Drawers built into risers must always be closed completely; otherwise, they become a tripping hazard.

LEFT Bookshelves follow this stairway to the second floor, the vertical dividers giving them more stability. Every other tread is illuminated, not only making the stairs safer but also highlighting the shelves.

FACING PAGE Because a stairway is traditionally placed near a front entrance, it makes sense to tuck a coat closet directly beneath it. The door to this closet is framed by the same rough-hewn beams used on the stair railings and ceiling.

RIGHT Following the diagonal lines of this stairway, custom cabinetry houses items ranging from small to large. This centrally located spot is the perfect place to keep oft-used items, such as a vacuum cleaner and other household essentials.

FAR RIGHT Like the stairs above them, these drawers are stepped. Suitable for everything from hats and scarves to table linens, the not-too-high drawers are easily accessible, too.

kitchens and dining

• • •

NOWHERE IN THE HOUSE WILL YOU FIND MORE BUILT-INS THAN IN the kitchen. Everyday activities—the prime among them being meal prep—require cabinets and shelves to house dishes, cookware, and, of course, food. The most prevalent built-in is the base cabinet; it not only houses all kinds of necessities but also supports countertops. Base cabinets aren't reserved for a kitchen's perimeter, either; kitchen islands are typically made up of counter-topped base cabinets with a built-in eating bar. Meanwhile, wall cabinets make the most of a kitchen's vertical space, especially if they reach all the way to the ceiling. Shelves may have a simpler appearance but that doesn't make them any less hardworking. Open shelves can make dinnerware easily accessible or keep much-used items close at hand. Shelves are a staple in a pantry as well.

Built-in dining options go beyond an island's eating bar. A corner of the kitchen might be reserved for casual dining or—in lieu of a conventional table and four chairs—a built-in banquette can serve for more formal occasions. Dining-related built-ins can go beyond the eating area per se. A hutch, corner cabinet, or sideboard can stand in for conventional storage pieces.

Finally, keep in mind that built-in appliances will affect the configuration of everything else. Whether it's a commercial-style stove in the kitchen or a wine refrigerator in the dining room, establish appliances' locations first and the rest will fall into place beautifully.

This built-in island is crafted to look like a piece of fine furniture but, at the same time, it's hardworking. In addition to a sink, sprawling counter, and drawer storage, it accommodates bar stools for a casual meal.

shape a kitchen with storage

● ● ● IT STANDS TO REASON THAT YOU'LL want as much built-in storage in your kitchen as possible, but don't hesitate to leave a little breathing room, too. A kitchen surrounded by base and wall cabinets, for instance, can hold plenty of kitchen essentials, but all that cabinetry can also make the space seem smaller from a visual point of view. Consider replacing some—or even all—of the wall cabinets with open shelves to create a more spacious feeling; if they're glass instead of solid wood, so much the better. Even glass-fronted cabinets create a more open and airy look than their solid-wood cousins.

Wall cabinets can, however, help define a kitchen's boundaries. Suspended from the ceiling, over-the-island cabinetry can demarcate the kitchen from the adjacent dining or family room.

Perimeter cabinets are largely responsible for defining the boundaries of this kitchen with the help of the built-in island, which adds both storage and informal seating.

ABOVE This kitchen, with a distinct Arts and Crafts style, relies on an island with varying heights and shapes to define its borders. Along one side, the countertop is stepped up and fitted with storage. Meanwhile, at the kitchen's edge, the countertop takes a turn, providing an eating area for two.

LEFT Fitted with doors and drawers of all sizes, this storage wall unquestionably separates the kitchen from the adjacent living area. Because a solid wall of cabinets might have been visually overwhelming, a cut-out niche offers a place for the eye to rest and provides valuable countertop space, too.

kitchen cabinets

●●● BEFORE SHOPPING FOR CABINETRY, TAKE inventory of what you'll be storing in it. That way, you'll have a place for everything, and you won't find out—too late—that your large dinner plates don't fit in standard 12-in.-deep wall cabinets. Stock wall cabinets are 30 in. high; if set at the suggested 15 in. to 18 in. above a standard 36-in.-high countertop, they won't reach the ceiling. The space above the wall cabinets might be used for display, or the ceiling can be dropped to make a soffit. But today it's more popular to take cabinets all the way to the ceiling, either by installing wall cabinets higher, ordering taller models, or stacking two cabinets on top of one another.

Kitchen base cabinets typically measure 34½ in. high to accommodate 1½-in. countertops. Of course, custom cabinets are an option, but a less expensive way of making your cabinets taller is to set standard cabinet cases on top of high-toe-space bases.

ABOVE On first glance, this china cupboard appears to be a piece of freestanding furniture. After closer inspection, though, it's clear that this is a built-in, recessed into the wall to take up less valuable floor space.

RIGHT Wall cabinets reach to the ceiling in this kitchen, leading the eye upward and making the room look taller. The crown molding of the cabinets matches the rest of the ceiling's trim, while base cabinets are decorative in their own right.

UNIVERSAL DESIGN DETAILS FOR CABINETS

universal design details are geared to make life easier for people of all ages and abilities. To make your cabinets more user friendly consider these details:

- Use full-extension glides on drawers and pull-out shelves.
- Opt for accessories that pull out, rotate, or swing out, especially for corner cabinets.
- In lieu of traditional wall cabinets, opt for open shelving lowered a few inches, or store the majority of your items in a pantry or in base cabinets.
- Make cabinet toe spaces deeper and taller, which will make it easier to negotiate with a wheelchair.
- Choose grab pulls instead of knobs and lever handles for full-height and pantry doors.
- Provide a seated workspace somewhere in the kitchen.
- Use glass door panels that let you see what's stored at a glance.

RIGHT As more people are aging in place, universal design makes more sense than ever. The aisles in this kitchen can accommodate a wheelchair, and all appliances are set at countertop level or below.

LEFT Conventional thinking calls for kitchen cabinets all in the same color, but this kitchen puts a new twist on tradition. The island and base cabinets are in a deep blue, providing visual weight. Meanwhile, white wall cabinets set against white subway tile all but disappear, making the room seem larger in the process.

•finding the right configuration

When configuring cabinetry, give some thought as to how you want your kitchen to work. Standard base and wall cabinets may completely meet your needs, but there are other options too; a tall china cabinet, perfect for serving pieces, might be located near the kitchen workspace yet be out of the way of the cook. Likewise, if the kids do their homework in the kitchen, a desk might be built in somewhere. Don't be concerned about perfectly lining up wall and base cabinets, either. Appliances and windows will invariably throw off the alignment. The good news is that a kitchen's backsplash, which provides a visual break, will make any less-than-perfect placement inconspicuous.

RIGHT An all-white approach gives this kitchen an open and airy look, but the cabinet configuration takes it to yet another level. Base cabinets do all of the heavy lifting here, while wall cabinets are limited to a pair—one set on each side of the cooktop.

TRASH AND COMPOST

a well-organized kitchen includes cabinets outfitted for trash, compost, and recycling. What type of containers you choose and where you locate them depends on your cooking habits. Contrary to what most people think, the cabinet under the sink is not the best place to put trash and recycling. Instead, locate pull-out garbage bins near food-prep areas, to the right or left of the wash-up sink. Another option is a trash bin attached to a door panel operated by a touch latch or, more simply, hooked open with your foot. Compost bins can be mounted under a countertop hole, as a pull-out, or even a built-in drawer, but they must be easy to remove, clean, and replace daily.

ABOVE If it's important to you to display dishes and serving pieces, glass-fronted cabinets and open shelves are your best bet. This kitchen even incorporates a china cabinet; located near the kitchen's edge, it's conveniently close yet outside of the primary work area.

RIGHT Representing a traditional approach to cabinet configuration, this kitchen features the full complement of door and drawer storage; a matching island even provides supplemental storage. Because all door and drawer fronts are solid and not see-through, the look is neat and orderly.

•fitting in appliances

When purchasing any appliance, it's important to coordinate the specifications with existing cabinets; be sure that doors can open fully, without interference from adjacent doors and drawers. A dishwasher positioned too close to a corner, for instance, might keep a drawer from opening.

Separate appliances may best serve some kitchens; in lieu of a conventional stove, for example, you might opt for a cooktop, one or more wall ovens, or even a specialized oven or two. Wall ovens can fit into a bank of cabinets or tuck under a countertop. Smaller ovens, such as microwave, steam, speed, and warming ovens, can fit into cabinetry above a wall oven but often function more comfortably when placed under the countertop.

ABOVE A single wall oven like this one should be placed so that the middle rack is at the user's elbow height, making it easy to move something from the oven to a nearby counter. Beneath this oven is a built-in cutting board, freeing up space.

RIGHT Refrigerator and freezer drawers tucked beneath the counter have the advantage of being easy to see and access, which means they also comply with universal design principles.

The placement of appliances is important in any kitchen, as the dishwasher here exemplifies. There's enough room to walk around it even with the door completely open, plus its proximity to the sink and cabinets where dishes are kept makes loading and unloading a breeze.

more about...
THE WORK TRIANGLE

he classic kitchen triangle consists of the range, the sink, and a refrigerator as its points. The legs of that imaginary triangle—the total distance between the three points—should add up to no more than 26 ft., though as few as 12 ft. is fine in a small kitchen. Think of those measurements as guidelines to make your kitchen its most efficient and to save you steps in the long run. Give careful thought to adjacent workspaces, too. In general, each appliance requires a landing space of about 15 in. You'll need a landing space near the refrigerator, and the sink will need 24 in. on each side, room for dirty dishes on one side and clean ones on the other. A cooktop requires both a landing space and prep area; they can be adjacent to the appliance or across the aisle—but no more than 4 ft. away.

LOCATING APPLIANCES

RANGES

The standard range is 30 in. wide, with four burners and a single oven. Some of today's models, though, feature a warming drawer or two stacked ovens; you'll also find side-by-side ovens in extrawide versions. Many professional-style ranges are taller and deeper than standard cabinetry. Consider setting stock cabinets on higher toe spaces to raise the countertop height and/or install them 1 in. or 2 in. away from the wall, which will allow deeper counters.

COOKTOPS

Cooktops can be installed into a countertop like a drop-in sink (with the countertop surrounding it on all sides) or like an apron-front sink (with the countertop interrupted by the unit). Take care that any backsplash behind a cooktop is resistant to heat as well as moisture and stains. Allow for a landing space that's at least 9 in. on one side and 15 in. on the other, with 9 in. behind the cooktop if it's on an island or peninsula. If there's bar seating behind the cooktop, provide at least 24 in. of space.

RANGE/COOKTOP VENT HOODS

A ducted vent draws cooking smells, smoke, moisture, and airborne grease away from the cooktop; grease is then captured while moisture and smoke are blown outside. A ductless hood vent filters grease and moisture, and then recirculates the air back into the kitchen. Built-in downdraft cooktop vents can pop up or be surface mounted. Pop-ups are better at venting than surface-mounted models, simply because they are physically closer to the tops of pots and pans. Both types of downdraft vents are less visible—and less expensive—than updraft vent hoods but may not be strong enough for high-intensity cooking. Venting an island will require a stronger fan than a cooktop against a wall, as the wall helps direct heat, moisture, and grease to the hood. A hood should ideally be about 3 in. wider than the cooktop to scoop air most effectively; it should be even wider on an island cooktop.

MICROWAVE OVENS

An over-the-range built-in microwave makes sense in a small kitchen. But in larger kitchens a better option is to tuck a built-in into a base cabinet, ideally at the end of a run of cabinets or in an island, away from the main cooking zone, especially if other family members tend to use the microwave while meals are being prepped. You can also give a freestanding model a built-in look by creating a custom niche in a base cabinet. Just be sure to provide an outlet at the back of the niche plus room for the cord.

WARMING OVENS/DRAWERS

A warming oven, also referred to as a warming drawer, can keep foods at an optimal temperature while the rest of dinner is being prepared. But they can serve more than their prime purpose. Warming drawers are also convenient for heating plates, proofing bread dough, defrosting food, and even drying breadcrumbs. A range with a built-in warming drawer can be an economical option, but consider convenience, too. A separate warming drawer can be positioned at a more comfortable level, such as just under the countertop.

REFRIGERATORS

Today, you'll find refrigerators that go beyond conventional, twin-bed-size appliances. Refrigerator drawers are increasingly popular, as are under-counter models. A standard freestanding refrigerator is typically 27 in. deep while stock cabinets are 24 in. deep, so the refrigerator will project 3 in. into the room. If that's not a look that appeals to you, consider a built-in refrigerator (an expensive alternative) or a freestanding cabinet-depth fridge. The shallow depth of these 24-in. refrigerators makes it easier to locate items but may also prevent the use of large platters. Still another option is to set stock cabinets 3 in. away from the wall to align with the front of a standard refrigerator.

WINE REFRIGERATORS

A built-in wine refrigerator (also called a wine cooler or wine chiller) is usually 24 in., the size of a dishwasher, and holds 28 to 60 bottles, depending on the size of the bottle. Most built-in models are stainless steel with glass-paneled doors, but—like standard refrigerators—some can be paneled to match the cabinetry. While built-in wine refrigerators vent out the front, freestanding models typically vent out the rear and thus should not be completely built into cabinetry. Finally, while a wine refrigerator located near the dining room can be a convenience, be aware that—like any refrigerator—it will make some noise.

DISHWASHERS

The standard dishwasher is 24 in. wide, although 18-in. models are available for tight spaces and extrawide dishwashers are also available. Whatever size you opt for, a dishwasher should be placed on one side or the other of the main sink, with dish storage nearby to make it a one-step process to load and empty. If you're considering dishwasher drawers, you can stack them or install one on each side of the sink. Separating the drawers means there's no need to bend over to unload the dishwasher, but installation will cost more due to additional plumbing and electrical work.

SINKS

The most versatile of sinks is a 33-in.-wide, 10-in.-deep single bowl, which is big enough for large cookie sheets and stockpots. Be aware that sinks with wide-radiused inside corners may look more spacious than they really are; their inside measurements may not be able to accommodate larger items. On the other hand, if every pot and pan goes straight into the dishwasher, a two-bowl sink may work just fine. Provide 2 ft. on each side of the main sink, one side for dirty dishes and the other for clean. Consider adding a prep sink too; an ideal location is close to the cooktop and the primary work surface, but it could be the centerpiece of a secondary prep area. Sinks can be mounted under the counter (undermount), integral with the countertop (for example, stainless steel or solid surface with no seams to clean), or dropped into the countertop.

Just as important as choosing a cooktop or range is the choice of the vent hood that will accompany it. For serious cooks, an updraft vent hood is a better choice than a downdraft; the latter may not be strong enough to draw all the smoke, moisture, and airborne grease away from the cooktop.

specialized storage

Kitchen cabinetry provides many an opportunity to make every square inch count. Running the gamut from spice drawers to lift-up or pull-out shelves—even wine closets—specialized storage can increase efficiency.

ABOVE To the right of the range, a pull-out cabinet holds spices and other everyday essentials, saving many a step for the cook. The sides on all three of the shelves are high enough to keep items from falling out but low enough to see the contents.

LEFT Located at the perimeter of the kitchen, this wine closet has more than convenience going for it. It's directly across from the island, which is a handy serving spot.

LEFT This cabinet has enough room for storage two tiers deep. Behind the top cabinet door, spices are kept in place with simple dowels. The spice rack swings open to reveal more pantry storage, the items easily accessible because there's nothing stacked in front of them.

When closed, this tall cabinet appears to be no more than a frame for the refrigerator. But it opens to reveal slim shelves just big enough to hold single rows of condiments, canned goods, and spices.

Adjacent to the kitchen, a temperature-controlled wine closet keeps favorite vintages close at hand. The glass-fronted door is a plus, too, allowing the owner to take inventory with one quick glance.

built-in islands

● ● ● THE BUILT-IN ISLAND HAS EVOLVED TO BE so much more than its predecessor, the simple kitchen table. Whether it's a cluster of cabinets capped with a countertop, creating an ample work surface, or includes appliances, a sink, and bar seating, a built-in island can be the model of efficiency. By no means are all islands just one level; a countertop might incorporate a standard-height food-prep area and a stepped-up eating bar. A three-level island isn't out of the ordinary, either, with specific zones for food prep and dining as well as a lower surface for, say, kneading bread, which is an ergonomically good choice.

An island can be as deep as you like, although less than 18 in. isn't useful for most tasks. On the other hand, if it's more than 5 ft. deep, you may have a tough time reaching the center. Consider any sink or appliances you plan to incorporate, as well as requisite plumbing, wiring, or ductwork. Built-in islands require electrical outlets at code-required locations, too, but that will make your island more efficient.

ABOVE This two-tier island keeps cooking and dining on different levels while incorporating plenty of storage. In front of the counter stools, cabinets house little-used items, and open shelves at one end of the island keep cookbooks within easy reach.

FACING PAGE This pale-blue island with carved feet gives the impression that it's a freestanding piece of furniture. The sink offers a clue that it's built in, given that plumbing is required.

ABOVE Although only a slim island will fit in this small kitchen, it's still quite useful. Because there is little counter space near the cooktop and ovens, the island serves as a dedicated landing spot and work area for the appliances.

In this otherwise all-white kitchen, an island made of reclaimed wood is the unquestionable star. There's something organic about it as well; because they're made of the same material, the island seems to grow right out of the floorboards.

m o r e   a b o u t . . .
SIZING UP ISLANDS

When deciding on the size of your kitchen island, the first consideration should be the amount of space between it and perimeter cabinets. A single-cook aisle can be 42 in. wide, but if there are typically two cooks working at once, a 46-in. to 60-in. aisle will be easier for both to navigate. A wider space is important when appliance doors open into the aisle.

Although the standard countertop height is 36 in., your island can be as low or as high as you like. Give some thought to what's most important to you: cooking, dining, or both, and keep in mind that you can have it all with a two-level countertop. Finally, in terms of placement, avoid interrupting two points of a kitchen's work triangle; you don't, for example, want to have to walk around your island to get from the sink to the refrigerator.

RIGHT Proof that islands need not be enormous, this island has just room enough to seat two. It uses the same elements as the surrounding cabinetry with a single exception: tapered legs give the built-in the look of finely crafted furniture.

BELOW An island can often be the best place for a sink, especially if it's positioned directly across from the range or cooktop. But this one incorporates a dishwasher and microwave, too, the latter placed at one end so family members can still use it while meals are being prepped.

built-in shelves

● ● ● ALL KINDS OF FOODS, COOKING TOOLS, and vessels can be good candidates for built-in shelves. And when it comes to sizing up shelves the general rule is that there are no rules; they can be any size at all.

Near the prep area, narrow shelves can accommodate spices and cooking oils, even wooden spoons and other utensils, while deeper shelves can hold larger—and lesser used—serving pieces as well as hefty cookbooks. Recessed shelves are an option, too, though they should be tucked into interior walls where insulation is not a concern. (See Chapter 2 on p. 34 for more information on sizing, spacing, and supporting shelves.)

While shelves can be any size, those positioned over countertops must be narrow enough to allow you to still work comfortably. For instance, over-the-counter shelves that are longer than 15 in. to 18 in. should be no deeper than 12 in. and should have sufficient lighting. The underside of an open shelf can be fitted with task lighting, with the front trimmed to conceal the fixture.

Although positioned directly over the countertop, these shelves are narrow enough to allow the cook to work comfortably. Shelves like these should be no more than 12 in. deep.

ABOVE Reclaimed wood teams up with marble to give this kitchen a look that's at once rustic and refined. Because an abundance of wooden wall cabinets could have been too much of a good thing, shelves take their place to the left of the range, keeping dishes and serving pieces within easy reach.

LEFT Open shelves line this pantry, their varied heights and widths accommodating everything from canned goods and staples to serving trays and small appliances. Baskets are a good solution for smaller items, keeping them neatly corralled.

pantries

●●● A PANTRY IS THE PERFECT SOLUTION to keep oft-used items out of sight but still conveniently close. A **cabinet** pantry, located within the kitchen's work triangle, can match the rest of the cabinetry, while the **reach-in** pantry is removed from the work triangle but has the same advantage of displaying its contents by opening a single door. If the reach-in pantry is shallow but wide, two doors are ideal; one wide door will swing too far out and a single standard door won't allow easy access. In both reach-in and **walk-in** pantries, shallow shelves (4 in. to 12 in. deep) high on the wall will allow you to see and store cans and jars; deeper 18-in. to 20-in. shelves for bulky items are best placed lower. A **butler's** pantry—between the kitchen and dining room—can also be fitted with the same cabinetry found in the kitchen. Its built-in countertop is handy as a secondary food-prep space, and it's often home to a small sink as well as secondary appliances, such as dishwashers, warming ovens, and under-counter refrigerators.

In this kitchen, side-by-side pull-out doors house handy pantries. Because each shelf has metal side supports, the contents within are both easy to see and in no danger of falling.

A barn-style door allows access to this home's walk-in pantry. Because the top half of the door is fitted with glass, it's easy to quickly take stock of the pantry's contents.

ABOVE The entrance to this walk-in pantry is fitted with a vintage-style door, its yellow color making it truly eye-catching. As a rule of thumb for walk-in pantries, 4-in.- to 12-in.-deep wall shelves allow you to easily see and store cans and jars; 18-in.- to 20-in.-deep shelves are best for bulky items, placed closer to the floor.

LEFT A set of barn doors gives this kitchen an unequivocal country look. But the architectural element has more than aesthetic value; the easy-to-open doors open to reveal a well-stocked pantry.

built-in dining

● ● ● THE POPULARITY OF BUILT-IN DINING IS on the rise; a cozy banquette in the kitchen or dining room is often a favorite place to eat. As for bar seating, it's easily accessible, and stools can be tucked away— or removed entirely—when the countertop is needed for food-prep or as a buffet space. Side-by-side seating is ideal for diners who want to chat with the cook, whereas L-shaped eating bars make for more camaraderie; diners can converse with ease and still see what's going on in the kitchen. Be sure, however, to think beyond sitting spots; built-in china cabinets and cupboards can further enhance your dining experience, keeping serving pieces close at hand.

An L-shaped banquette tucks into the corner of this kitchen, with storage drawers built in below. The drawers could be difficult to access were it not for the fact that the freestanding table can be easily moved.

ABOVE The simplicity of this table and chairs allows a built-in china cabinet to be the unquestionable focal point of the dining area. Stretching from floor to ceiling, the storage piece takes advantage of every vertical inch.

LEFT This china cabinet is recessed into the wall, a particularly good strategy in small spaces. It provides just as much storage as a freestanding piece would without taking up an extra inch of valuable floor space.

LEFT Providing continuity from the nearby kitchen—where base and wall cabinets are, respectively, deep blue and white—these built-ins are perfectly suited for a dining room. There's plenty of drawer storage for table linens, while glass-fronted wall cabinets showcase fine china.

ABOVE Built-in dining also encompasses eating bars. This one, stepped up from the island's work surface, is perfect for a casual meal. The bar stools can quickly be removed, however, when buffet space is needed.

RIGHT A bank of recessed cabinetry in this formal dining room is large enough to keep all of the necessities in one spot. The built-ins have just a hint of whimsy too; glass-fronted cabinets are backed with fanciful black-and-white wallpaper.

Set between a bank of tall cabinets and an exterior wall, built-in seating in this kitchen has a comfy, cozy feeling. A magnetic chalkboard above the banquette adds a touch of playfulness; it's an ideal place to write reminders, to list chores, or even to practice spelling and math.

more about...
THE IMPORTANCE OF ELBOW ROOM

t o allow ample space for a seated diner, the National Kitchen & Bath Association[SM] recommends 32 in. between the table or countertop edge and the nearest vertical wall or obstruction—if no through traffic passes behind the diner. If, however, traffic does pass behind the seated diner, that dimension should be increased to 44 in., or 36 in. if you don't mind squeezing. For countertop height, depth, and width, see the chart below.

	COUNTER HEIGHT	KNEE-SPACE DEPTH	WIDTH PER SEAT	SEAT HEIGHT
Table dining	28 in. to 30 in.	18 in.	24 in.	18 in. to 19 in.
Standard countertop height	36 in.	15 in.	24 in.	24 in. to 26 in.
Bar height	42 in.	12 in.	24 in.	30 in.
Universal design access for wheelchair	27 in. to 34 in.	17 in. at feet; 11 in. at knees	36 in.	N/A

living areas

● ● ●

AS LIVING AREAS—ENCOMPASSING DENS, FAMILY ROOMS, AND LIVING rooms—are becoming more casual, they're also becoming home to a wider range of activities. Built-ins are a good match for many of those pursuits, but where they truly excel is in shaping space and adding style.

In terms of shaping and defining space, a single built-in can create an impressive focal point for a room. A fireplace, a television—or a combination of the two—might be the focus of the main seating group. And built-in bookshelves on either side can be designed separately or as part of a single unit that also encompasses the fireplace and TV. More often than not, built-ins are placed against interior walls, although tall cabinets flanking a window might inspire a cozy built-in bench between them.

Likewise, built-ins are a natural when it comes to establishing, or reinforcing, a certain style. In a traditional-style home, classically detailed built-ins can disguise the trappings of modern-day living; today's wealth of electronics can simply be hidden behind closed doors. Likewise, built-ins are key in retaining a contemporary home's streamlined look, quietly storing all kinds of belongings.

Narrow shelves flank a window in this living area, providing display space without blocking the natural light from coming in. Because the shelves are so narrow, collectibles are limited, but that gives them more emphasis.

Undoubtedly, part of the appeal of built-ins—especially in living areas—is the cozy feeling they can provide; ceiling-reaching built-ins can wrap a room in comfort. To keep multiple built-ins from feeling heavy, however, mix solid-door cabinets with their glass-door counterparts, and add some shelves along the way.

make a space multipurpose

●●● BUILT-INS ARE RIGHT AT HOME IN LIVING areas. Think through how your public spaces are used before deciding which built-ins are best for you. For many homeowners, a living area is the primary place to entertain family and friends, so a built-in bar might be in order. For others, it's where the family gathers to watch television; built-in cabinetry can be crafted to conceal the TV or not.

Storage is especially important and can be customized to fit your needs. If there are avid readers in the house, built-in bookcases may be a part of your plan. If you have small children—and toys are often spread out on the floor—you'll likely want some kind of cabinet to corral the clutter at the end of the day. From game boards to TV trays, whatever you regularly use in a living room should have a home there.

Closed storage lines a wall of this living room, providing a place for everything from dinnerware and linens for the nearby dining area to toys and games in the lower cabinets, where they're easily reachable by kids.

LEFT Tucked into one corner of a room where entertaining is the primary purpose, this built-in bar makes good use of what could have been an underused area. The fact that it's well out of the way of the living area's main traffic patterns makes it even more attractive for congregating.

BELOW A stone fireplace is the unquestionable focal point in this living room. Its visual weight could have been overpowering in the otherwise all-white space were it not for the similarly sized built-in storage unit to the left.

make personal style a priority

● ● ● THE BEAUTY OF BUILT-INS IS THAT YOU can customize them to the nth degree; they can be just as simple or as ornate as you like. They can take on the look of a freestanding piece of furniture. A traditionalist, for instance, might take a cue from a favorite chest or cabinet after studying the details that distinguish it. By adding similar elements—and differentiating the baseboard from the surrounding walls—you'll get the look of your own custom piece.

On the other hand, built-ins can blend seamlessly into your home's architecture, a real plus in a contemporary home. By exactly matching a built-in's baseboard and trim to the rest of the room's architectural features, it will look as though the piece had been there from the very day the house was built.

At the far end of this modern living area, a built-in bench provides a casual sitting spot with open and closed storage underneath. Over the bench, a flat-screen TV is installed low enough for comfortable viewing but high enough so that no one seated will hit his or her head.

ABOVE At first glance, it's evident that these homeowners appreciate modern art. Thus it's no surprise that they've transformed their fireplace into a work of art in its own right. Although the molding is traditional in style, the ombré facade gives the fireplace a contemporary twist.

LEFT Built-ins can cover all the bases, no matter what your personal style may be. In this rustic chic living room, a stone fireplace—with a flat-screen TV above—takes center stage. To the right, white-painted display shelves define the stairway, and to the left, brown-stained closed storage blends quietly with the room's overall color scheme.

organize
electronics

● ● ● IT GOES ALMOST WITHOUT SAYING THAT today's home electronics take up a fraction of the space their predecessors did. Tube-style televisions have been replaced with flat-screen TVs, and multicomponent stereos have given way to much smaller sound systems. Technology is unpredictable and ever changing, so when designing storage for your electronics, it's best to plan for some flexibility. For instance, vinyl albums had all but completely disappeared, but they've recently seen a resurgence and thus turntables have as well.

Although TVs have built-in speakers, many homeowners prefer to connect their sets to external speakers for surround sound. Front speakers can be built right into cabinetry, as can side and rear speakers. Unless you're proficient with electronics though, it's wise to hire a professional consultant when designing built-ins for complex audiovisual equipment. Finally, no matter how large or small your components are, keep in mind they'll require space for power cables and ventilation as well as easy-to-access storage for remote controls.

The built-ins in this living room are understatedly elegant. The TV is underscored by cabinetry with cut-outs that accommodate ottomans; the upholstered pieces can be paired with nearby chairs or rolled anywhere in the room.

ABOVE Open shelving gives easy access to electronic components in this living room and provides plenty of ventilation. More systems today are wireless, although many audiophiles believe wired speakers are superior. If a wired system is your choice, keep in mind it may require a more complex built-in design.

RIGHT AND FAR RIGHT Taking advantage of a hearth with some height, electronic components are housed inconspicuously behind a see-through door. Here, or anywhere electronics are enclosed, ventilation is extremely important.

•fitting in the television

As traditional living areas morph into informal spaces, more and more TVs are right at home there, sometimes sharing the spotlight with the fireplace or, just as often, serving as the sole focal point.

Installing a flat-screen television directly on the wall is one option, but built-in cabinetry has the advantage of adding architectural interest. Plus it makes wiring easier to conceal. Within built-in cabinets, a flat-screen TV can be stand-mounted or wall-mounted. A stand mount is simpler; the TV simply rests on a

shelf or counter. A wall-mount, on the other hand, can be installed in a custom-size niche.

If you're building from scratch, be sure blocking is added between studs where any flat-screen television may be installed; 3/4-in. plywood is often attached between studs in the general area where a television will be. Existing drywall can be cut out and replaced with plywood. Opening up the wall also makes it easier to run cables behind the finish surface.

LEFT Built-ins to the left of the fireplace in this living room house a large-screen television in the center section. While all of the doors have push latches, the doors that conceal the TV can slide back out of the way.

FACING PAGE TOP A niche in this living room accommodates both the fireplace and a flat-screen TV, one just as minimalistic as the other. Built-in bookshelves on each side are simple in their styling; their symmetry adds to the room's sense of serenity.

more about...

TV PLACEMENT

a flat-screen television that's mounted within a built-in cabinet can be a good solution when the sightline is ideal and the cabinet sides aren't too deep. But if you plan to view the TV from various places in the room or if the TV is installed higher than your sightline, consider a tilting or articulating mounting bracket. These types of brackets allow you to tilt the TV down to avoid glare or make for easier viewing throughout the room.

Likewise, they allow you to pull a TV out from the inside of a cabinet. Check your product's literature for the range of motion and for any restrictions on the television's size and weight. Flat-screen TVs are much thinner than their tube predecessors but they can still be hefty, so it's important to use any safety restraints that come with the television, especially if there are young children in the house.

The closer the television is to the viewer, the more important it is to locate the television at a comfortable viewing height. If the TV must be higher than recommended, install it on hardware that allows the TV to tilt toward viewers.

Distance recommendations vary widely:
- 5 ft. to 8 ft. for a 32-in. TV
- 6 ft. to 12 ft. for a 42-in. TV
- 8 ft. to 14 ft. for a 60-in. TV

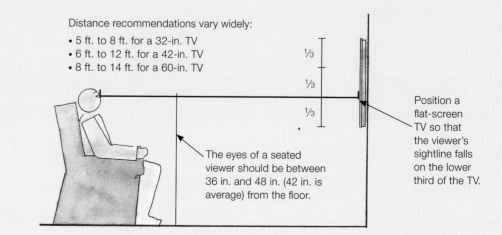

The eyes of a seated viewer should be between 36 in. and 48 in. (42 in. is average) from the floor.

Position a flat-screen TV so that the viewer's sightline falls on the lower third of the TV.

more about...

PLACING A TV OVER A FIREPLACE

i nstalling a television over a fireplace can result in a single, impressive focal point. Some challenges come with the territory, though. Check your TV's product literature to see if there are any recommendations for over-the-fireplace placement; in some cases, the warranty could be voided. Keep in mind that a television placed over a fireplace with a tall opening or substantial hearth may be too high for comfortable viewing. Plus a masonry chimney will make a TV more difficult to mount and make it tough to conceal the wiring.

When watching television isn't on the agenda, this barn-style door—finished to match the surrounding walls—slides to the far left, completely covering the TV screen and the shelves above it. When a favorite program comes on, though, the door moves effortlessly out of the way.

ABOVE In this vaulted living room, a modern storage unit—with the center shelf reserved for a TV—stops just short of a decorative window, which draws the eye instantly to the built-in's striking design.

LEFT Because this flat-screen TV is tucked into a niche, it's blocked from much of the light coming from windows on either side of the room, thus cutting down on glare.

m o r e   a b o u t . . .
CONCEALING THE TELEVISION

h omeowners who prefer to conceal their TVs behind closed doors have several options. Until recently, media cabinets often featured pocket doors that opened out and then slid back into the cabinet. Built-ins fitted with these doors are less popular today, though, because they require more depth than a flat-screen TV needs. Instead, sliding doors have come into vogue; when open, they cover shelves on each side of the television. Other options include standard hinged doors, folding hinged doors, and a single barn-style sliding door.

focus on the fireplace

● ● ● THE FOCAL POINT OF MANY A LIVING area is the fireplace, whether it's a streamlined contemporary version or a traditional type that lends architectural interest to the room. The appeal of a fireplace is more than visual; there's a warm and welcoming aspect that makes it the unequivocal heart of the home. What's more, the mantel can provide display space, and niches for firewood and tools can be handsome additions.

There's much to be said for the roaring flames—and aroma—of a wood-burning fireplace, but gas-burning and electric fireplaces have their advantages, too. They don't require chopped wood (that has to be hauled through the house) and can often be started with a flip of a switch. Whatever type of fireplace you opt for, however, safety should be a primary concern. Always check with local building officials to make sure your design meets all codes and ordinances.

This stacked stone fireplace in varying shades of gray could have given the room a country vibe. Instead, a crisp white mantel and smart-looking shelves to the left result in a much more traditional and tailored appearance.

ABOVE The mix of materials used in this fireplace wall is as dazzling as its design. A minimalistic mantel is just deep enough to hold treasured photos and collectibles, while the equally unpretentious hearth underscores built-in shelves to the right.

LEFT When crafting a fireplace from an exquisite material, like the marble used for this traditional example, it's smart to keep the overall design simple so the substance itself is showcased.

BELOW Wall-to-wall built-ins in this living room include not only a fireplace but cabinets and shelves, too. Like many fireplaces, this one features mesh curtains to protect against flying sparks and rolling embers, while bifold doors add an extra element of safety.

ABOVE In a living room otherwise decked out in pale neutral hues, a jet-black fireplace is the star attraction. Because its facade is three-dimensional, and the nearby bookshelves are recessed, the architectural element takes on even more importance.

FACING PAGE BOTTOM There's a Zen-like feeling to this living room, where an extended hearth has plenty of room for seat cushions on each side of the fireplace. A jagged-edge piece of marble serves as the mantel; blending quietly into the backdrop, it furthers the feeling of tranquility.

provide display space

● ● ● WHILE THE OVERALL DESIGN OF A ROOM can speak volumes about your personality, so can the treasures within. Showcasing books, family photos, artwork, and collectibles can give guests a clue as to what—and whom—you hold dear. Plus keeping these items out in the open allows you to appreciate them on a daily basis.

Built-in shelves can blend quietly with the rest of the room; if they're finished with like details and colors, the objects on display get more importance. Or take the opposite tack with a built-in that stands out as a key piece in its own right, fashioned with contrasting material. Yet another alternative is to opt for the best of both worlds. Match a built-in cabinet's side and front surfaces to the rest of the room but choose a contrasting color for the interiors. In a white-painted built-in, for instance, a dark interior can add depth and make light objects pop.

If wallpapering an entire room seems a bit overwhelming, consider papering the backs of bookshelves instead. These built-ins are decked out in a spirited pattern that's in keeping with the living room's cheery disposition.

BELOW In this living room, white-painted cabinetry pairs up with wood-stained shelves, giving them separate-but-equal status. Deep shelves like these are best for the display of photos and art objects, which require enough space so they're not in danger of falling.

ABOVE While many built-in shelves are made of wood, glass has its own advantages. The material's more delicate nature keeps showcased collectibles to a minimum, putting focused importance on each. Plus accent lighting can be positioned so it shines through all of the shelves.

RIGHT In a white-painted built-in like the one in this living room, a darker interior can add depth while making light objects pop. A collection of blue-and-white pottery is showcased here, as are the silver-framed photos.

BELOW These homeowners took advantage of a deep exterior wall to build in tall-and-narrow display space. Because the shelves are carved out in triplicate, their dramatic impact is just as impressive as the view beyond the room's windows.

LEFT While most built-ins seem to be linear in style—with square or rectangular framework— this recessed version takes a more graceful approach, thanks to its arched design and the light that shines down softly.

BELOW A doorway in this traditional home features an extra-thick wall, providing sufficient space for display shelves and closed storage below. The built-ins not only make efficient use of available space but also lend a sense of continuity between two rooms.

workspaces

• • •

WHETHER IT'S AN AREA FOR THE KIDS TO SPREAD OUT THEIR HOME-work or a dedicated office for someone who works from home, a workspace is a necessity in every residence. A desk is invariably the centerpiece, where a computer often dictates the size of the surface; a laptop requires less space than a full-size desktop computer. And, if you're not planning to fit your printer into a nearby cabinet or shelves, you'll need to reserve room for it on your desktop, too.

Built-in shelves are practical for even the smallest workspace, and a multitude of different-size drawers can hold everything from pencils and erasers to printer cartridges and reams of paper. File drawers are essential too, especially for the telecommuter who needs to organize information by topic, company, or client. Built-in storage is a particularly good choice for heavy file folders; their sheer weight could cause a freestanding cabinet to tip over. Likewise, a workspace should be set up ergonomically to suit all users, whether they're full-time or part-time.

A well-planned workspace can make room for hobbies too. If you're an arts and crafts aficionado, reserve a corner of the desk—as well as several drawers and shelves—for your favorite pastime. If you use the workspace more for hobbies than for hard work, you may want to reverse the designated spaces.

Just a few steps inside the entry of this residence, a built-in desk tucks into an alcove. Although it has a small footprint, the workspace has plenty of closed storage as well as display shelves and, for a chic touch, leather handles on the doors and drawers.

configuring your workspace

● ● ● THE MOST EFFICIENT WORKSPACE STARTS with a list of its requirements. In terms of office equipment, printers run a close second to computers. But because their dimensions can vary greatly, some will need more space than others. An all-in-one printer, for instance, may be bigger, but on the upside it can handle printing, faxing, copying, and scanning. Whatever model you choose will need clearance above to operate it and on the sides to clear paper jams. Although a printer can be set on a stationary shelf, a pull-out shelf—in a base cabinet or deep shelving unit—will allow easier access for operating and troubleshooting. Keep in mind, too, that full-extension slides are a necessity for any pull-out shelf.

A well-organized work area also requires plenty of storage, both open shelves and closed cabinetry. To accommodate oversize books and binders, shelves in workspaces are typically deeper than, say, in the living room. Likewise, they should be strong enough to adequately carry the weight.

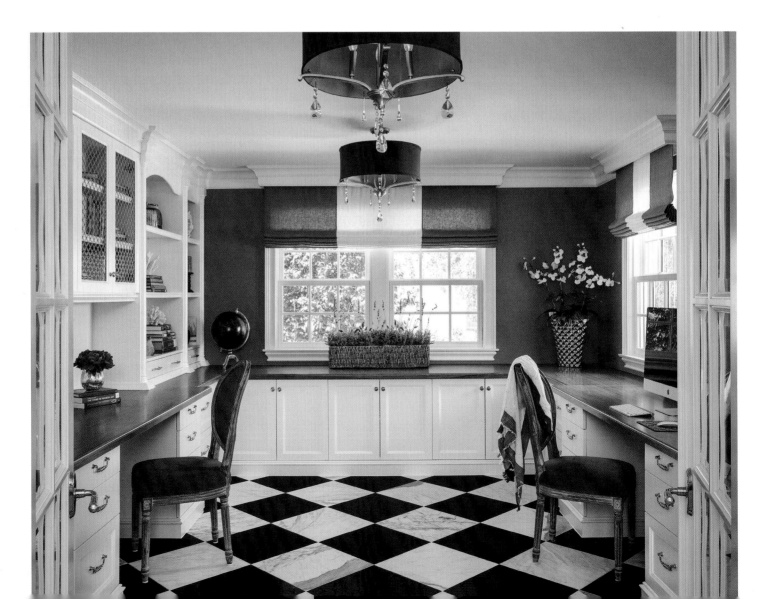

LEFT Open shelves can keep things organized and within easy reach, but just because they are basic doesn't mean they have to be boring. In this feminine take on a home office, shelves are primarily backed in a soft blue hue, with one here and there in pale pink, picking up on the painted radiator and accent table.

ABOVE Matching the rest of the room's architecture to a tee, built-in storage in this home office blends quietly into the backdrop, allowing the handsome desk and armchair to take the spotlight. The neutral surround allows items on the shelves to stand out prominently.

FACING PAGE This dedicated home office easily accommodates two people, or one person going back and forth between two tasks. On one side of the room, an uninterrupted countertop allows plenty of room to spread out while working at the computer. On the other side is a supplementary workspace plus above-the-counter storage for office essentials.

RIGHT An architectural niche created by two columns is the perfect place for a built-in desk in this living area. Because the workspace tucks back between the columns, it's less obtrusive.

RIGHT When space is at a premium and school-age children want to work on crafts or homework at the same time, one desk that accommodates all can be the perfect solution. This wall-hung desk, with a single support leg, features built-in lights and a bulletin board, perfect for showing off creations the kids are proud of.

ORGANIZING CABLES

Like any cabinet intended for electronics, those that house computer components require space for cables and ventilation. If space allows, install stock cabinets a few inches from the wall, freeing up space to run cables. Precut holes in drawer and cabinet backs where necessary, and position one or more grommet holes in the desktop; cable-management troughs can keep cables tidy.

Another solution is to keep cables and uninterrupted power supply (UPS) strips tucked against the back wall, concealing them with a removable panel several inches from the back wall (see below).

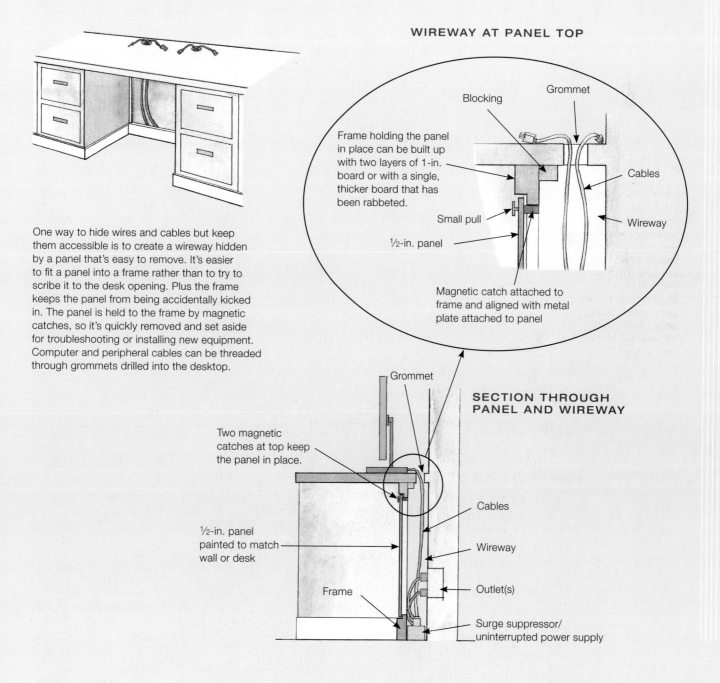

DESK WITH PANEL REMOVED

One way to hide wires and cables but keep them accessible is to create a wireway hidden by a panel that's easy to remove. It's easier to fit a panel into a frame rather than to try to scribe it to the desk opening. Plus the frame keeps the panel from being accidentally kicked in. The panel is held to the frame by magnetic catches, so it's quickly removed and set aside for troubleshooting or installing new equipment. Computer and peripheral cables can be threaded through grommets drilled into the desktop.

WIREWAY AT PANEL TOP

Blocking

Grommet

Frame holding the panel in place can be built up with two layers of 1-in. board or with a single, thicker board that has been rabbeted.

Cables

Small pull

Wireway

½-in. panel

Magnetic catch attached to frame and aligned with metal plate attached to panel

SECTION THROUGH PANEL AND WIREWAY

Grommet

Two magnetic catches at top keep the panel in place.

½-in. panel painted to match wall or desk

Cables

Wireway

Frame

Outlet(s)

Surge suppressor/ uninterrupted power supply

sizing your workspace

●●● DEPENDING ON WHAT YOU WANT TO accomplish, a workspace can take up the entire room or just a sliver of that space. A family member who works full-time from home will no doubt need a dedicated area, complete with plenty of storage and bookshelves. Likewise, an avid crafter may want a room completely devoted to his or her hobby. In either scenario, a workspace in full view of a home's public areas should be able to be closed off with a conventional, pocket, or sliding door; that way, you won't feel compelled to put materials away mid-project.

On the other end of the spectrum, you may need a workspace no more than a few feet wide— just large enough to accommodate a laptop and paperwork on one or both sides. Tucking a desk into a kitchen or great room is one option, but think outside the box, too. You might, for instance, carve out a workspace from under a stairway or use some dead space at the end of a hall.

Built-ins are straightforward in this home office, with open shelves above the countertop and closed storage below. In front of the window, there's room enough for a desktop computer, which is a real plus; this way, it doesn't take up valuable space on the nearby desk.

ABOVE In any home office, papers and projects can quickly make a mess of a desktop. Here, though, an abundance of storage makes it easy to keep things neat and tidy. Drawers keep files and small items in order, while overhead doors conceal books and binders. Open shelves are also handy for often-used items, such as reference materials.

BELOW Not everyone needs a dedicated home office; sometimes just a slice of space will do. In this family room, one end of a storage wall is reserved for a desk, with shelves above and a printer to the right. On the opposite end of the built-in, bookshelves house titles for both business and pleasure.

ABOVE What could have been a mere pass-through has been transformed into a multipurpose place. A desk for two—made up of nothing more than a countertop and file cabinets—rounds the corner at the far end of the space. Built-in seating and to-the-ceiling storage face one another.

m o r e   a b o u t . . .
ERGONOMICS

a full-time home office should be designed with ergonomics in mind, but it's just as easy—
and important—to apply the same principles to a part-time workspace.

Most desks are designed too high for comfortable keyboarding. It's important that—while
looking straight ahead—you're focused squarely on the computer screen or, at the very least,
your head is tilted down slightly. Elbows should be bent at 90°, perhaps a bit more but no less.
A lower desk can make computer work more comfortable or a keyboard can be positioned on
a pull-out surface just beneath the desktop. Likewise, a laptop can be set on a pull-out tray.

Those who work primarily on a laptop may also find it comfortable to work while standing,
so built-in cabinets that accommodate sitting and standing positions can offer flexibility. For
example, a comfortable working height for a 5-ft. 6-in. person is 25 in. while seated and 40 in.
when standing. Thus a keyboard tray should be a positioned a bit lower than specified, so the
keyboard itself is 25 in. high.

LEFT A long and narrow room can be a challenge, but these homeowners turned theirs into an asset. A cantilevered desk provides plenty of surface to spread out work, butting up to a floor-to-ceiling cabinet. Meanwhile, shelves on the opposite wall keep books and binders within arm's reach.

BELOW This built-in desk is perfectly suited for a young child. Below the desktop, doors and drawers are at his or her level (although they could be lockable). The desktop itself is covered with glass—making it easy to clean—and open shelves keep selected items out of reach.

creating a craft area

The ever-increasing popularity of home sewing, arts, and crafts has translated to workspaces of all sizes dedicated to hobbies. The right built-ins can keep you organized and make it easier to complete tasks. Specifically, off-the shelf closet systems like the one in this room can be precisely customized to your needs.

Customized for a sewing and craft room, this storage system incorporates space to stash fabrics and notions as well as a laptop and, of course, a sewing machine.

ABOVE Wire drawers are a good choice for a sewing room; they allow you to see fabrics at a glance. Because they're see-through, wire drawers also encourage you to keep things orderly.

RIGHT This storage system turns a corner, extending into an adjacent room. The custom compartments hold a fold-down table, a microwave, and even a small refrigerator. The unit is just tall enough to clear the ceiling beam that separates the two spaces.

LEFT Until needed, a sewing surface stays discreetly behind tall cupboard doors. In a matter of minutes, however, it can be pulled down— ready to accommodate the next project.

BELOW Opposite the wall that's devoted to fabrics and notions, adjustable shelving, an easy DIY project, keeps small items organized with the help of baskets and bins.

bedrooms and closets

● ● ●

IT'S THE FIRST PLACE YOU SEE EVERY MORNING AND THE LAST PLACE you see each night, so the bedroom should be the epitome of comfort, and built-ins can go a long way toward that goal. That starts with the bed itself. A built-in headboard can make a dramatic, eye-catching statement, while built-in night tables and shelves on each side can keep bedside necessities within easy reach. Built-ins can even provide cozy comfort in a child's room; bunk beds can be a smart—and space-saving—solution, especially for two kids who share a space.

The opportunities for built-ins in the bedroom go far beyond beds. Built-ins for bed linens are a natural, while a cozy window seat can be peaceful and serene while providing storage below. And, of course, there's the closet, a bedroom's primary built-in. A standard reach-in closet fitted with rods, shelves, and drawers can meet your clothes storage needs efficiently. Given the luxury of more space, though, you may want to opt for a walk-in closet or dressing room.

Finally, if you're one of the many people who use the bedroom as an around-the-clock retreat, it's important to give careful thought as to how you'll use yours.

A conventional bed tucks into built-in cabinetry that creates a custom niche for the sleeping spot. Cantilevered bedside tables are part of the contemporary design, complete with adjustable lighting.

Whether you're an at-home worker who requires a desk all hours of the day or someone who jumps on a laptop an hour or two each night, a work surface can be built in to meet your needs. Or maybe your priority is more leisurely pursuits; a big-screen TV and audio equipment can be built in opposite the bed. The bottom line is this: No matter what your needs may be, built-ins are one of the best ways to meet them.

add architectural interest

● ● ● IF YOUR BEDROOM IS NOT MUCH MORE than a big, square box, take heart. Built-ins not only can serve functional purposes but also can add architectural interest. Think of your room as a blank canvas and start by arranging the furniture you have—perhaps the bed, a dresser, and a pair of night tables. From there, fill in the blanks; give some thought to the room's other necessities. Maybe you could use more storage space or a display unit that will also house a flat-screen TV. Building those essentials into your space is sure to increase its practicality as well as its aesthetic appeal.

While built-ins can add architectural interest to an otherwise-plain bedroom, you might also find the reverse is true. Because bedrooms are often on the second floor, you may find architectural elements that you'll need to work around. You might tuck shelves or a workspace under a sloped ceiling. Likewise, a gable dormer could provide the ideal place for a cozy window seat.

These homeowners made the most of a second-story bedroom, where gables and a fireplace were already in place. Built-in bookshelves flank the fireplace—also creating a mantel—while, on an adjacent wall, a cozy built-in seat nestles beneath a pair of windows.

LEFT A fireplace adds architectural interest to any room, but this traditional version gets a modern twist. Above the mantel, a niche has been carved out to accommodate a flat-screen TV.

ABOVE In this master bedroom, an existing fireplace resulted in nooks on either side, creating alcoves perfectly suited for built-in seating.

LEFT A built-in headboard gives this bed focal-point prominence, but surrounding cabinetry takes it a step further. In lieu of conventional nightstands, drawers on each side of the sleeping spot hold bedside necessities while shelves above house an entire library of nighttime reading.

built-in beds

● ● ● THE CENTERPIECE OF THE BEDROOM— the bed itself—can be built in as easily as anything else. It may be elaborate, surrounded by bookshelves and storage, or as simple as a custom-crafted platform bed with a night table attached on each side.

In fact, creating custom night tables gives you the opportunity to determine how much space you really need. If you're an avid reader, you'll need room for books, magazines, maybe even an electronic reader. (Be sure there's a charging station nearby; you might want to build one into the night table's drawer.) Plus you'll need space for a bedside lamp as well as a clock and/or your smartphone.

A built-in headboard is another option; an upholstered headboard, in particular, can make an ideal backrest for reading in bed or watching TV. And don't forget about under-the-bed space; it can be used for built-in drawers, a great place for out-of-season clothing.

Proof that bunk beds need not be reserved just for kids, these take on a more sophisticated air—perfect guest quarters for older teens or even adults. Floor-to-ceiling curtains can be pulled for privacy but, in case anyone feels claustrophobic, there are windows fitted with lights at the end of each bunk.

ABOVE An impressive built-in bed takes center stage in this master bedroom. The platform style is just as understated as the built-in wall behind it, which incorporates bedside lamps as well as electrical outlets for charging cellphones and tablets.

LEFT Sleeping bunks don't always have to be stacked, demonstrated in this dormered room. Here, bunks are placed end-to-end, with a privacy wall between them and built-in storage below.

more about...
WALL BEDS

the ultimate built-in bed is one that, until needed, is tucked away into a wall or storage unit—a space-saving alternative for a studio apartment or a guest room that doubles as a den or home office. It's often referred to as a Murphy bed, although that's a proprietary name for a particular wall-bed manufacturer. There are other brands on the market, including DIY kits, and, of course, you can have a wall bed custom built.

built-in cabinetry

●●● CUSTOM CABINETS CAN MAKE YOUR bedroom the ultimate retreat. Whether you're looking for an entertainment center to accommodate all of the latest technology or shelves that can hold books along with treasures you want to display, built-ins are often the best solution.

Where you locate your built-ins can make a big difference. Try to position built-in cabinetry on interior walls; if you have two bedrooms next to each other or a bedroom adjacent to a hallway, strategically placed built-ins can provide sound insulation. Similarly, built-in cabinets positioned on the wall between the master bedroom and bathroom make sense; they create a clear visual barrier. If the built-ins are used for clothes storage, however, add a door to separate the two rooms, as clothing should not be frequently exposed to humidity.

ABOVE If you have trouble finding the perfect piece of furniture, a built-in can be the best solution. This dresser takes advantage of every available inch, measuring as wide as possible without interfering with the window and as deep as possible without blocking the door.

RIGHT These homeowners found themselves with a dilemma as to where to place the TV without interfering with the stunning view beyond the window wall. The solution, as it turned out, was quite simple; the TV—operated remotely—drops down from the ceiling.

ABOVE AND RIGHT Built-ins in this bedroom start with the bed itself (above) backed by a tufted headboard that serves as a backrest, too. Meanwhile, surrounding cabinetry incorporates storage space that includes bedside tables. On the opposite side of the room (right), an entire wall of storage matches that around the bed, interrupted only by a niche reserved for a flat-screen TV.

ABOVE AND LEFT
Because the trimwork of these cabinets (above) exactly matches that of the windows above them, the combined elements look like one focal-point piece. In addition to providing conventional storage, there's a surprise, too; with the touch of a button, a flat-screen TV pops up from behind the center doors (left).

RIGHT Working with a round window and a sharply angled ceiling might have been too much of an undertaking for many, but these homeowners met the challenge head on. The vanity follows the curve of the window, while built-in drawers—set on bun feet to look like furniture—rise just to the point at which the ceiling starts to angle.

BELOW A bench is convenient in any dressing area, providing a place to sit down while putting on socks and shoes. This one goes the extra mile, though, by providing drawer storage that matches the rest of the cabinetry in the room.

built-in closets

●●● WITHOUT A DOUBT THE BEDROOM'S most functional built-in, a closet can take several forms. The standard 2-ft. reach-in closet can work beautifully, especially if it's outfitted to suit your specific needs.

There should be space for both short and long articles of clothing as well as drawers and open shelves (see "Sizing Up a Clothes Closet" on p. 139).

If you need more space, a walk-in closet or, even bigger, dressing room may be the answer. Either can be designed in a variety of configurations. The latter typically has room for a full-length mirror as well as an ironing board and iron, plus a bench where you can sit to change shoes. There might even be a built-in island in the center, made up of drawers and a countertop.

An added benefit of a walk-in closet or dressing room is that you can close the door for privacy. If space is tight or if you want to avoid a door swing, pocket doors can be a good option.

ABOVE This sleek, streamlined dressing area features his and her sides, providing space for hanging and folded clothing behind closed doors. Even the central island accommodates a couple; drawers on both sides keep small items in order.

RIGHT Good lighting is important in any dressing room, so one with natural light is preferable. The fact that this one also has a chandelier—providing ambient light—is a bonus.

To tailor a dressing room to your specific needs, start by taking inventory of the clothing you already have and allow for a few additions. This gentleman's dressing room includes stacked drawers approximately the same height as a bachelor's chest.

ABOVE These storage drawers, specifically tailored for a man's closet, keep cuff links and collar stays organized in the top drawer, with ties and pocket squares neatly folded in the drawer below.

LEFT From the marble-topped island to a luxe chandelier to the smart-looking hardware and matching hangers, this dressing room looks more like a high-end retail shop than a personal changing area. It offers proof, once again, that the difference is often in the details.

more about...
CLOSET SYSTEMS

One of the best ways to stay organized is with a closet system, which can be retrofit into an existing closet or be part of a custom design. Home-design stores and online closet companies alike offer a wealth of after-market accessories that can accommodate entire wardrobes.

Off-the-shelf closet systems can range from ready-to-install to semicustom, with parts sized to precisely what you need. Closet systems are also available in a wide range of materials. Wire shelving is relatively inexpensive and easy to install. It works well for shoes, hats, boxes, and hanging clothes, but folded clothing set on wire shelves will soon develop grid

marks, so a sturdy shelf liner is required. Panel-product shelving (particleboard or medium-density fiberboard, either painted or finished with a surface such as melamine) tends to be more expensive than wire but has a more traditional look and is easier on folded clothing. Closet systems made primarily of wood are available, too, and can often be budget friendly.

Several companies offer online or in-store design services for very low fees or even free of charge. And while some systems are designed and installed by the manufacturer, others are delivered to you and installed by a third party—or you, if you're handy.

SIZING UP A CLOTHES CLOSET

The top shelf can be ideal for odd-shaped items such as hats and boots and for out-of-season storage. If the closet door is the standard 6-ft. 8-in. high, this shelf must be shallow enough to allow you to reach past it to store bulky items.

The centerline of the upper rod should be 40 in. to 42 in. from the centerline of the lower rod.

A rod for dresses and coats can be as low as 66 in. above the floor, but raising it higher provides boot or shoe storage below. Hanging storage typically requires a depth of at least 2 ft., although coats may require a 28-in. depth.

Shelves for folded clothing should be 12 in. apart and 16 in. deep.

Shoe shelves should be 6 in. to 7 in. apart and 12 in. to 16 in. deep.

A 42-in. rod height is best for shirts, skirts, suits, and folded pants.

Closed storage in 16-in.-deep drawers is ideal for underwear, hosiery, and other small items. Drawer dividers can help items stay organized.

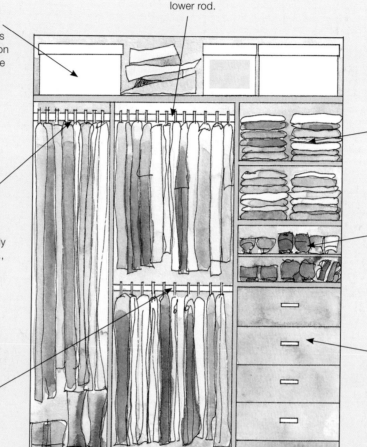

These narrow drawers are perfectly suited for storing small items, but it's the dividers within those drawers that do the heavy lifting by organizing everything from billfolds and pocket change to watches and other jewelry.

A sliding barn-style door is the perfect solution in a small space, as it doesn't require clearance for a door swing. The hardware for this one protrudes far enough that the door clears the artwork to the right too.

CREATING A
CUSTOM CLOSET

there's no written rule that closets must be limited to one level; sometimes there's nowhere to go but up. This two-level closet/dressing room is the perfect example. It makes the most of every inch, with the upper level perfectly suited for off-season storage.

TOP LEFT To the right of the staircase, a tall cabinet—complete with an eye-level mirrored back—is flanked by shoe storage, the shelves varied in height to accommodate different styles of footwear.

BOTTOM LEFT The vast height of this space allows enough room for a second level, accessed by a staircase with handrails on each side for safety's sake. A hamper is tucked under the staircase, conveniently placed near the adjacent bathroom.

ABOVE For the most part, hanging clothes in this closet are on easily reachable rods. Special pieces, though, are protected behind mirrored doors that double as a looking glass.

built-ins for kids' rooms

●●● BUILT-INS CAN PROVIDE SMART STORAGE in kids' rooms, keeping everything from clothes to toys in order. In terms of closets, overall flexibility is key. A mix of pegs, hooks, and hangers is a good idea for kids just old enough to put clothes away, but as they grow, more rod space will be needed for longer wardrobes. Drawers are handy at any age for small items like socks and underwear, but consider built-in shelves for folded clothes, which allow kids to see the contents at a glance.

Small children also need lots of space to store toys and games, so opt for built-ins that encourage keeping things neat. Because the floor is often the ideal play area, keep storage low so it can be reached. Open shelves can be fitted with soft-sided bins that can hold a wide variety of items and be pulled out safely. Older children can benefit from open shelves too. But because they're not as apt to pinch their fingers, the shelves—taller, of course—might well be mixed with closed storage.

Built-ins are the order of the day in this boy's room, where a built-out wall features a niche just big enough for the bed—suspended by rods at the foot—with recessed shelves on either side. More recessed shelves are set into an adjacent wall for some of the occupant's favorite books and toys.

ABOVE Because small children need lots of space to store toys and games, both open and closed storage are optimal. In this play space, closed storage is low and reachable, although doors and drawers might be lockable. Another safety measure: Be sure that a TV is attached securely to the wall, so it can't be pulled down on someone.

ABOVE Bright colors and lively patterns are the order of the day in this playroom, nowhere more so than in built-in storage units. Solid turquoise-painted doors mix it up with white doors, their circular cut-outs revealing a vivid orange that matches the cabinetry's hardware.

LEFT Children often feel a sense of adventure when climbing a ladder to get to their sleeping quarters. Because this room's occupant is still rather young, the ladder is short for safety's sake. The elevated bed still allows room, though, for plenty of closed storage below.

gallery

bunk beds

Whether two or more kids share a room or sleepovers happen on a regular basis, bunk beds can be the perfect solution in a child's room.

Most bunks stack twin beds atop one another, but this set takes a different tack. A twin-size bed with a safety rail is on top, while a full-size bed is on the bottom.

ABOVE Though it appears to be suspended from ropes, the bottom bunk in this boy's room is set on legs. The top bunk, on the other hand, is cantilevered from the wall with rope playing a supporting role in its stability. Appropriately, a rope ladder—firmly secured at both top and bottom—provides access to the top bunk.

ABOVE Built-ins are everywhere in this boy's room. The top bunk is accessed via the staircase (just out of view to the right), while the bottom bunk can simply be climbed into. Plus, to the left of the beds, there's plenty of built-in seating.

LEFT This bedroom makes the most of a long-and-narrow attic space. End-to-end bunks line the two side walls—with drawer storage below—leaving plenty of play space in between.

bathrooms and laundry rooms

• • •

MUCH AS KITCHENS ARE GREATLY DEPENDENT ON BUILT-INS, bathrooms are too; they provide comfort and convenience at every turn. Even the most basic bathroom includes a sink built into a vanity, a medicine cabinet, and a tub, stand-alone shower, or a combination of the two. A fully decked-out master bath might house a separate water closet, a soaking tub, a luxuriously large shower, a full-height linen closet, and extensive cabinetry.

Shelf storage, however, is important as well. Deep shelf storage works well for towels and washcloths, while shallow shelves might be more appropriate for toiletries and other small items. An alternative to offering two depths of shelving is to use deep shelves throughout; toiletries can be corralled in baskets or bins. Likewise, small items might be allocated to deep-cabinet storage, again stored in baskets or bins. Be sure, however, that those cabinets are fitted with pull-out shelves.

Even small built-ins can make a big difference in a bathroom, like a shampoo niche built into the shower wall or a single shelf to display a potted plant. And don't forget to build in hooks and towel bars. Hooks by the shower or bath provide a great place to temporarily hang towels, but in order for them to dry completely, they should be moved to a bar.

There's something spa-like about walking through a set of French doors to be greeted by a luxurious tub located straight ahead. This one features built-in shelves on each end, keeping bath linens close at hand.

Laundry areas are sometimes built into a bathroom, but more often than not have a dedicated space. Built-in cabinets are well suited for hampers, detergents, and other laundry essentials. Even the washer and dryer themselves can be quietly built into a laundry room's framework.

bathroom built-ins

●●● IN ADDITION TO SUPPORTING A bathroom's essentials, well-placed built-ins can establish privacy and tranquility. Privacy, for instance, is particularly important when it comes to the toilet, especially if you don't have a separate water closet. But if there's enough space between, say, the vanity and the toilet, a floor-to-ceiling linen closet between the two might provide the perfect partition. Likewise, oversize showers and tubs can impart a sense of serenity; just be sure they're positioned to give you all the privacy you desire. There's even a certain sense of calm that comes from having your own sink. Two sinks with a shared cabinet between them can ease morning and nighttime bathroom routines for a couple.

Universal design elements are highly desirable in a bathroom as well; a cantilevered sink (that a wheelchair can fit under), sturdy grab bars at the toilet and shower, and pull-out shelves in cabinetry all add to the level of comfort. For guidelines on where to place bathroom built-ins, see the drawing on p. 151.

a bathroom, like any other room, should have three types of lighting: task lighting for grooming, ambient lighting for overall illumination, and accent lighting for highlighting textures or details. And it's important to consider the placement of all three when designing built-ins in your bathroom. At the sink, wall-mounted sconces, vertical lights, or even pendant lights—placed close to eye level on each side of the mirror—are ideal for task lighting. For ambient lighting, a pendant or surface-mounted light in the center of the room can bounce light off the ceiling and walls. Finally, for accent lighting, small spotlights are often the best solution.

ABOVE Simplicity can sometimes be the best solution, proven in this bathroom. A black-and-white scheme takes its cue from the whimsical wallpaper, with a cultured stone countertop echoing the dark neutral. Meanwhile, built-in storage is carried out in crisp white. An above-the-counter cabinet is especially handy: Its top section is fitted with shelves for easy access.

RIGHT A wide variety of textures and materials gives this master bath its eye-catching appeal. But its beauty is more than skin deep; there's also plenty of practical allure. A cantilevered vanity like this works well for universal design; it's easy to pull a wheelchair up to it.

FACING PAGE A soaking tub fits under a bay window in this luxuriously large bathroom, creating an undeniable focal point. But just as impressive are twin vanities, featuring open and closed storage below their countertops and mirrored-to-the-ceiling cabinetry above.

more about...
TOILETS

t he ultimate necessity in a bathroom, the toilet can prove to be awkward when it comes to placement. Even if space is tight, try to position it so it's not the first thing that you see when you open the door. If space allows, consider locating the toilet in a separate room, preferably with a small sink. That said, a toilet placed behind a partition can work just about as well.

A wall-hung toilet leaves the floor free for easy cleaning but costs more than a standard pedestal toilet. Also, a wall-mounted model with an in-wall tank requires a thicker-than-standard wall. Finally, keep in mind that the space above a toilet can be a prime place for storage; a shallow cabinet can work well here as can open shelves.

ABOVE AND LEFT This master bath is strategically planned, allowing two people to use the space at the same time. Each sink has its own shelf—handy for fresh towels—and there's drawer storage within easy reach (left). To the left of the vanity, a built-in linen closet keeps more bathroom essentials close while partitioning off the toilet (above). It also provides a little privacy for someone toweling off after stepping out of the shower.

SIZING UP BATHROOM BUILT-INS

the dimensions given in the drawings are those generally suggested by the National Kitchen & Bath Association. Keep in mind, however, that minimal dimensions are often smaller and those recommended for universal design are often larger.

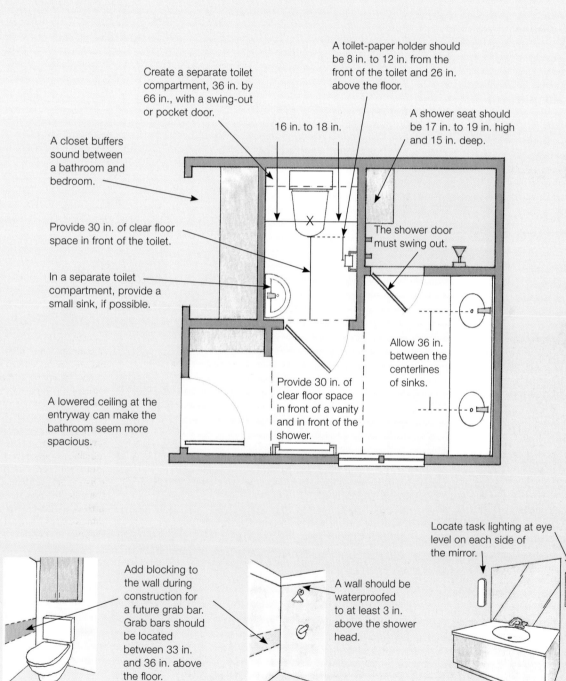

A toilet-paper holder should be 8 in. to 12 in. from the front of the toilet and 26 in. above the floor.

Create a separate toilet compartment, 36 in. by 66 in., with a swing-out or pocket door.

16 in. to 18 in.

A shower seat should be 17 in. to 19 in. high and 15 in. deep.

A closet buffers sound between a bathroom and bedroom.

Provide 30 in. of clear floor space in front of the toilet.

The shower door must swing out.

In a separate toilet compartment, provide a small sink, if possible.

Provide 30 in. of clear floor space in front of a vanity and in front of the shower.

Allow 36 in. between the centerlines of sinks.

A lowered ceiling at the entryway can make the bathroom seem more spacious.

Add blocking to the wall during construction for a future grab bar. Grab bars should be located between 33 in. and 36 in. above the floor.

A wall should be waterproofed to at least 3 in. above the shower head.

Locate task lighting at eye level on each side of the mirror.

vanities

● ● ● THE MOST COMMON CABINET IN A bathroom is a vanity, which provides storage space and supports the sink. The height of your vanity should be based on your height as well as the type of sink you're using. A vessel sink, which is set atop the counter, requires that the vanity be positioned lower than if you choose an undermount, integral, or drop-in sink. Most vanities are between 30 in. and 32 in. high, although if someone tall uses the bathroom, a vanity with a standard sink might be more comfortable at 36 in. high. A vanity can also be hung like any other wall cabinet, off the floor completely. This requires careful coordination with the plumber early on, but on the upside, the resulting clearance makes it easy to clean under the cabinet and to pull a wheelchair up to it.

Vanity cabinets typically run from 18 in. to 24 in. deep; the depth is determined by the size of your sink as well as the overall space available in the bathroom. To increase the amount of storage space, top the vanity with one or more wall cabinets that extend all the way to the ceiling.

RIGHT This vanity reaches from one wall to the other, but with carved feet, it looks more like a piece of furniture that's been custom-made to slide into the niche. The medicine cabinet is recessed into an adjacent wall.

RIGHT Emerald-green glass countertops make a splash in this bathroom; their striking color is a crisp contrast for the pure white vanities. Because each vanity has plenty of open and closed storage, there's less of a need for conventional medicine cabinets; adjustable mirrors are used here instead.

This vanity accommodates two people in a single niche. Individual medicine cabinets provide his and her mirrors. And, although plumbing is exposed below the countertop, there's still plenty of space on open shelves to keep toiletries close at hand.

more about...
MEDICINE CABINETS

t he shallow shelves that a medicine cabinet provides can be an asset to a bathroom; it's the perfect place for small toiletries as well as grooming supplies. If plumbing pipes aren't in the way, a medicine cabinet can be recessed into the wall over a vanity sink. Otherwise, it will have to be surface-mounted. Another option is to locate the medicine cabinet on a nearby wall and center a plain mirror on the wall over the sink.

If a medicine cabinet is truly used to store medicine, be sure—for safety's sake—that it's lockable, placed high on the wall, or both.

ABOVE This contemporary bath owes much of its clean-lined appeal to the vanity, with an extra-thick white counter and contrasting wood drawers. The fact that the vanity is set on legs and the drawers don't go all the way to the floor makes the room look open and airy.

RIGHT These two vanities are located on adjacent walls—and not side by side—so it's easier for two people to get ready at the same time without tripping over one another.

LEFT Because the toekick matches the dark stone floor, the lighter, marble-topped vanity seems to float on air. A toekick also has a practical purpose; it allows you to stand closer to the sink and mirror.

BELOW Although bathrooms are often thought of as sleek and streamlined, there's no reason they can't have a traditional look. This one takes a cue from Victorian times, especially the vanity with its gingerbread details.

sinks

●●● THE BATHROOM SINK, SOMETIMES referred to as a lavatory, can take many shapes and sizes. Pedestal sinks are ideal for small spaces, such as powder rooms, but they don't offer vanity-cabinet storage. They are, however, a good choice if you need wheelchair access.

Self-rimming sinks can fit into any countertop material. Undermount sinks, though, require monolithic countertop materials. Because the edge of the countertop is exposed, consider stone, solid surface, composite, or cast concrete. Vessel sinks, too, run the gamut of shape, material, color, and size. Keep in mind, however, that a vessel sink requires coordination between the cabinet height and depth and the fixture type and location; it must be positioned properly to be comfortable to use.

Sink placement is just as important as the sink choice. A couple on the same morning schedule might share a bathroom with two sinks, but this layout works best if the bathroom is compartmentalized, with, at the least, the toilet in a separate space.

Inspired by the communal sinks used in the early days of indoor plumbing, the trough sink—like this contemporary incarnation—has come a long way. It makes the most of minimal space, a real plus in this long and narrow bathroom.

LEFT A pedestal sink is ideal for small spaces like this boy's bathroom, but the downside is that it doesn't have vanity-cabinet storage. That problem is solved beautifully here, however, with storage cabinets on each side that reach to the windowsills.

ABOVE This vessel sink features delicate curves, which, in turn, inspired the soft lines of the hardware and mirror. A low-profile sink like this is best used by adults, who aren't as apt to spill water over the sides as are youngsters.

LEFT Vessel sinks can take many shapes and forms. This hammered-copper bowl perfectly suits the rustic wood-paneled bathroom and matching vanity. Copper light fixtures and hardware further play up the sink's metal finish.

tubs and showers

● ● ● ALTHOUGH MANY NEW HOMES AND remodels feature stand-alone showers and separate soaking tubs, a bathtub fitted with a shower is still a popular option. If you are shopping for a tub to use as a shower too, look for one with a wide, not-too-tall tub with a close-to-flat bottom that's easy to step into and stand up in while taking a shower.

If your tub has a deck and surround, those elements need to be waterproofed in some way. They can be wrapped in tile or covered with stone, solid-surface, or a composite that's been cut or molded to receive a self-rimming or undermount tub. Keep in mind, however, that tubs with water jets or other powered features require some kind of side-access panel.

Provide plenty of space for towels and toiletries, too. Open shelves or cubbies at the end of the tub—even niches carved into the wall—provide built-in storage solutions that are just as practical as they are good looking.

A freestanding tub is typically the focal point of a bathroom, but here the dramatic impact is doubled. The tub is set in front of a fireplace, positioned high enough for a bather to have a good view.

To create a sense of continuity, the same white subway tiles used on these bathroom walls dress the facade of the tub, too. That simple notion allows the marble deck to stand out more prominently, just like the finger tiles that back the built-in niches.

ABOVE AND BELOW This beautifully designed bath looks more like a room full of high-end furniture than a utilitarian space. Matching vanities, with marble waterfall countertops, are positioned on opposite walls (above), leading the eye to a freestanding tub at the far end of the room. The vanity on the right backs up to a luxuriously large shower (below) interrupted—almost imperceptibly—by a mirror over the sink.

ABOVE This tub/shower design is intertwined, creating a single, smart-looking unit. The shower surround overlaps the tub's deck and, in turn, the tub's deck steps down to provide a seat in the shower.

•shower enclosures

As a rule, a shower is a much more practical choice than a soaking tub, as a tub gets a fraction of the use that a shower does. Shower-only stalls can be as small as 32 in. square, but it's worth it to add even 6 in. to 10 in. to each dimension for an extra element of comfort.

A typical shower has a curb with a shower door at minimum, and glazed panels where the shower isn't surrounded by solid walls. One-piece and sectional molded shower stalls are available for quick, watertight installation, although tile combined with glass enclosures offers endless style possibilities. Glass shower enclosures can be frameless, which show off a shower's fittings and wall finishes, or framed, which are generally less expensive and offer a sturdier look.

What type of shower surround you choose also depends on the shower itself. A steam shower, for instance, requires an enclosure that completely seals off the shower stall. And the European-style "wet room" features a shower with no curb; the area just beyond the shower is meant to get wet, or at least damp, during a shower.

LEFT Because this glass shower enclosure is frameless, it shows off the shower's fittings and finishes. But it goes a step further. This European-style wet room has no door or curb, which means the bathroom is likely to get wet, or at least damp, beyond the shower entry; this layout, however, is a good option for universal design.

LEFT This master bath has the luxury of a separate tub and shower; the tub fits neatly into an alcove, while the shower gets a nearby corner all to itself. The tub has a navy-blue backsplash, but the shower takes the color to another level. Its frameless surround shows off the walls' navy hue.

ABOVE Taking design inspiration from the home's architecture, this master bath is traditional to the nth degree. The tub is set low enough beneath a bank of windows to provide privacy, but it's in the shower where the difference is in the details. Support beams reach to the ceiling's crown molding, while half-walls provide an element of privacy.

laundry rooms

●●● LAUNDRY TASKS CAN BE A LITTLE LESS daunting with just a little forethought. For starters, locate laundry facilities near bedrooms and bathrooms, if possible. Or, at a minimum, create a dedicated niche in the bathroom for laundry baskets, where dirty clothes can be collected.

Every laundry area, whether it's a dedicated room or not, should provide space to sort, a surface on which to fold, rods for hanging shirts just taken from the dryer, a high shelf for laundry supplies, and a place to store an ironing board and iron. A front-load washer next to a companion front-load dryer automatically creates folding space on top of the two machines, although installing a continuous countertop over the units will create a smoother surface. On the other hand, a stacked washer and dryer might allow space for a storage cabinet to one side and a countertop for folding on the other.

ABOVE LEFT AND RIGHT A deep sink in a laundry room is convenient for delicate, hand-wash items; it's even better if there's nearby counter space where they can lay flat to dry (right). The real stars in this space, though, are the washer and dryer. The tall front-loading machines mean you don't have to bend or stoop, making it easier on your back (left).

ABOVE Stackable units make the most of this laundry area, which doubles as a pantry. Given the washer/dryer's small footprint, there's plenty of room for storage space, which can be used for everything from laundry supplies to staples.

RIGHT Every necessity is covered in this laundry room; in addition to plenty of cabinetry, there's a sink and a rod from which to hang shirts. There's even a countertop over the washer and dryer, providing a place to fold clothes.

In this multipurpose laundry room, a vintage-looking farmhouse sink stands ready for hand-washing delicates or arranging fresh flowers. Meanwhile, the nearby washer and dryer slide in under a custom countertop, which provides a flat working surface. Cabinets above keep detergents and other laundry essentials safely out of the way.

ABOVE In this laundry area, a single wall accommodates every need. A stacked washer and dryer are out of the way at the far end of the room, while a rod over the sink is perfectly positioned for hanging shirts. Because counter space is limited, there's a pull-out surface for folding clothes.

ABOVE Just around the corner from the kitchen, this laundry area uses the same cabinetry, creating a cohesive look from room to room. Base cabinets—their countertop perfect for folding clothes—tuck between a stacked washer and dryer on one end and a tall closet on the other.

ABOVE The countertop over this washer and dryer is deeper than the surface surrounding the nearby sink. That allows space for required ventilation and ductwork in back of the machines and, at the same time, provides a larger working surface.

photo credits

p. ii-iii: Mark Lohman, design: Jennifer See

p. 2-3: Mark Lohman; Ryann Ford, design: CG&S Design-Build; Eric Roth, design: Paul Krueger, AIA, Krueger Associates (left to right)

CHAPTER 1

p. 4: Mark Lohman

p. 6: Trent Bell Photography for Winkelman Architecture

p. 7: Mark Lohman (top left, bottom), design: Alison Kandler Interior Design; Ryann Ford (top right), design: Mark Cravotta/Cravotta Interiors, David Webber/Webber + Studio Architects; builder: Redbud Construction Co.

p. 8: Mark Lohman (left), design: Alison Kandler Interior Design; Stacey Bass (right), design: Jay Levy Architects, styled by Yvonne Claveloux

p. 9: Mark Lohman (top), design: Alison Kandler Interior Design; Hulya Kolabas (bottom)

p. 10: Chris Luker/Collinstock, design: Dixon/Kirby Homes

p. 11: Trent Bell Photography for Peterson Design Group Architecture and Derek Preble (top); Mark Lohman (bottom)

CHAPTER 2

p. 12: Mark Lohman, design: Alison Kandler Interior Design

p. 14: Hulya Kolabas (left); Mark Lohman (right)

p. 15: Joanne Kellar Bouknight

p. 16: Trent Bell Photography for ARQ Architects (left); Mark Lohman (right), design: Alison Kandler Interior Design

p. 17: Brian Vanden Brink, design: Hutker Architects

p. 18: Trent Bell Photography for Derek Preble (top); Kathryn Russell (bottom), design: Alison Kandler Interior Design

p. 19: Mark Lohman, design: Jennifer See

p. 20: Kathryn Russell, design: Alison Kandler Interior Design

p. 21; Ryann Ford (top), design: Amity Worrel & Co.; Ryann Ford (bottom), design: Mark Cravotta/Cravotta Interiors

p. 22: Chipper Hatter (top), design: Model Design Inc.; Ryann Ford (bottom), design: Anita Joyce/Cedar Hill Farmhouse

p. 23: Joanne Kellar Bouknight (top); Andrea Rugg Photography for Otogawa-Anschel Design + Build (bottom)

p. 24: Eric Roth (top); Hulya Kolabas (bottom), design: Michelle Hogue/Hogue Interior Design

p. 25: Hulya Kolabas (top), design: Michelle Hogue/Hogue Interior Design; Andrea Rugg Photography for Otogawa-Anschel Design + Build (bottom)

p. 26: Susan Teare (left), design: Silver Maple Construction; Rob Karosis/Collinstock (right), design: Randy Trainor/C. Randolph Trainor Interiors

p. 27: Rob Karosis/Collinstock (top left), design: Janice Page, PKsurroundings; Jo-Anne Richards (top right), design: Ines Hanl/The Sky is the Limit; Rob Karosis/Collinstock (bottom left), design: Knickerbocker Group; Mark Lohman (bottom right)

p. 28: Mark Lohman (left), design: Alison Kandler Interior Design; Emily Followill Photography/Collinstock (right), design: Urban Grace Interiors; builder: Benecki Fine Homes

p. 29: Tria Giovan

p. 30: Emily Followill Photography/Collinstock, design: Melanie Milner/The Design Atelier, Greg Busch Architects, AIA

p. 31: Tria Giovan (left), design: Amanda Nisbet; Jim Westphalen/Collinstock (top right), design: Birdseye Design; builder: Roundtree Construction; Andrea Rugg Photography for West Bay Homes (bottom right)

p. 32: Susan Teare, design: Cushman Design Group; builder: Conner & Buck Builders

p. 33: Trent Bell Photography for Urban Dwellings (top); Eric Roth (bottom): design: Olson Lewis Architects, Ken Dietz Interiors

p. 34: Emily Followill Photography/Collinstock (top), design: T. Duffy & Associates; Joanne Kellar Bouknight (bottom)

p. 35: Ryann Ford (top), design: Amity Worrel & Co.; builder: J.C. Schmeil; Trent Bell Photography for Nicola's Home and Elizabeth Moss Galleries (bottom)

p. 36: Ken Gutmaker (left), design: Mike Schulte; Mark Lohman (right), design: Alison Kandler Interior Design

p. 37: Emily Followill Photography/Collinstock, design: Jessica Bradley Interiors

CHAPTER 3

p. 38: Mark Lohman, design: Alison Kandler Interior Design

p. 40: Tria Giovan

p. 41: Ryann Ford (top), design: Amity Worrel & Co.; Andrea Rugg Photography/Collinstock (bottom), design: Rosemary Merrill Design, Jen Seeger Design

p. 42: Tria Giovan (top), design: Phoebe Howard; Trent Bell Photography for Taylor Interior Design (bottom)

p. 87: Trent Bell Photography for Peterson Design Group Architecture and Derek Preble (top); Kathryn Russell (bottom), design: Alison Kandler Interior Design

p. 88: Andrea Rugg Photography for Otogawa-Anschel Design + Build (left); Hulya Kolabas (right), design: Michelle Hogue/Hogue Interior Design

p. 89: Brian Vanden Brink (left), design: Hutker Architects; Mark Lohman (right), design: Alison Kandler Interior Design

p. 90: Chipper Hatter, design: Model Design Inc.

p. 91: Andrea Rugg Photography (top), design: Liz Schupanitz Designs; Kathryn Russell (bottom left, bottom right), design: Alison Kandler Interior Design

p. 92: Trent Bell Photography for McMahon Architects (top); Mark Lohman (bottom), design: Alison Kandler Interior Design

p. 93; Eric Roth, design: Ruhl Walker Architects

CHAPTER 6

p. 94: Hulya Kolabas

p. 96: Chipper Hatter, design: Model Design Inc.

p. 97: Brian Vanden Brink (top, bottom), design: Polhemus Savery DaSilva Architects

p. 98: Trent Bell Photography for GO Logic

p. 99: Hulya Kolabas (top), design: Michelle Hogue/Hogue Interior Design; Mark Lohman (bottom)

p. 100: Mark Lohman, design: Richard Turner Architect

p. 101: Brian Vanden Brink (top), design: Adolfo Perez Architect; Mark Lohman (bottom left, bottom right)

p. 102: Mark Lohman

p. 103: Eric Roth (top), design: Sea-Dar Construction; Joanne Kellar Bouknight (bottom)

p. 104: Tria Giovan, design: Kate Jackson

p. 105: Tria Giovan (left), design: John Bjornen; Mark Lohman (right), design: Noelle Schoop/Carrie Mapes

p. 106: Stacey Bass, design: Raquel Garcia Design

p. 107: Trent Bell Photography for Hacin + Associates (top); Hulya Kolabas (bottom), design: Stacey Gendelman Designs

p. 108: Susan Teare (left), design: Peregrine Design/Build; Hulya Kolabas (right)

p. 109; Brian Vanden Brink (bottom), design: Hutker Architects

p. 110: Mark Lohman, design: Alison Kandler Interior Design

p. 111: Hulya Kolabas (left); Eric Roth (right), design: Adams + Beasley Associates

p. 112; Tria Giovan (top), design: Greg Shano Interiors; Hulya Kolabas (bottom), design: Tirmizi Campbell

p. 113: Ryann Ford (top left); Eric Roth (right), Shepard Construction and Development

CHAPTER 7

p. 114: Eric Roth, design: Elisa Allen Interior Design

p. 116: Chipper Hatter, design: Model Design Inc.

p. 117: Eric Roth (left), design: Ruhl Walker Architects; Hulya Kolabas (right)

p. 118: Chipper Hatter (top), design: Model Design Inc.; Hulya Kolabas (bottom), design: Michelle Hogue/Hogue Interior Design

p. 119: Joanne Kellar Bouknight

p. 120: Kathryn Russell, design: Alison Kandler Interior Design

p. 121: John Olson (top); Eric Roth (bottom left), design: Siemasko + Verbridge; Andrea Rugg Photography for Otogawa-Anschel Design + Build (bottom right)

p. 122: Mark Lohman, design: Alison Kandler Interior Design

p. 123: Trent Bell Photography for Caleb Johnson Architects (left); Mark Lohman (right), design: Alison Kandler Interior Design

p. 124: Mark Lohman

p. 125: Mark Lohman

CHAPTER 8

p. 126: Ryann Ford

p. 128: Brian Vanden Brink, design: Polhemus Savery DaSilva Architects

p. 129: Hulya Kolabas (top); Tria Giovan (bottom left), design: Phoebe Howard; Mark Lohman (bottom right), design: Alison Kandler Interior Design

p. 130: Tria Giovan, design: Phillip Sides

p. 131: Eric Roth (top), design: Adolfo Perez Architect; Stacey Bass (bottom), design: Allison Caccoma/Caccoma Interiors

p. 132: Mark Lohman (left), design: Alison Kandler Interior Design; Chipper Hatter (right), design: Myca Loar, Shiny Bones Design

p. 133: Eric Roth (top, bottom), design: Adams + Beasley Associates

p. 134: Andrea Rugg Photography/ Collinstock (top, bottom), design: Cobblestone Homes

p. 135: Eric Roth (left), design: AbbeyK; Tria Giovan (right), design: Nancy Taylor